THE POWER
OF THE
BLESSING

THE POWER OF THE BLESSING

5 Keys to Improving Your Relationships

John Trent, Gary Smalley, and Kari Trent Stageberg

W PUBLISHING GROUP

AN IMPRINT OF THOMAS NELSON

Portions of this book were abridged from: *The Blessing* © 2019, 2023 John Trent and Kari Trent Stageberg, revised edition 978-0-7852-2905-6 and © 1986, 1993, 2011 Gary Smalley and John Trent, 978-0-7852-6084-4.

Published in Nashville, Tennessee, by W Publishing Group, an imprint of Thomas Nelson.

Thomas Nelson titles may be purchased in bulk for educational, business, fund-raising, or sales promotional use. For information, please email SpecialMarkets@ThomasNelson.com.

Unless otherwise noted, Scripture quotations are taken from the New King James Version®. © 1982 by Thomas Nelson. Used by permission. All rights reserved.

Scripture quotations marked THE MESSAGE are from THE MESSAGE. Copyright © 1993, 2002, 2018 by Eugene H. Peterson. Used by permission of NavPress. All rights reserved. Represented by Tyndale House Publishers, a Division of Tyndale House Ministries.

Scripture quotations marked NASB are from the New American Standard Bible® (NASB). Copyright © 1960, 1962, 1963, 1968, 1971, 1972, 1973, 1975, 1977, 1995, 2020 by The Lockman Foundation. Used by permission. www. Lockman.org

Scripture quotations marked NIV are from the Holy Bible, New International Version®, NIV®. © 1973, 1978, 1984, 2011 by Biblica, Inc.® Used by permission of Zondervan. All rights reserved worldwide. The "NIV" and "New International Version" are trademarks registered in the United States Patent and Trademark Office by Biblica, Inc.®

Scripture quotations marked NLT are from the Holy Bible, New Living Translation. Copyright © 1996, 2004, 2015 by Tyndale House Foundation. Used by permission of Tyndale House Ministries, Carol Stream, Illinois 60188. All rights reserved.

Scripture quotation attributed to the J. B. Phillips translation is from The New Testament in Modern English by J. B. Phillips. Copyright © 1960, 1972 J. B. Phillips. Administered by The Archbishops' Council of the Church of England. Used by permission.

Names have been changed to protect the identities of people referred to in this book.

978-1-4003-3877-1 (TP)
978-1-4003-3878-8 (epub)
978-1-4003-3879-5 (audiobook)

Library of Congress Cataloging-in-Publication Data

Trent, John, 1952–
The blessing: giving the gift of unconditional love and acceptance / John Trent and Gary Smalley. — Rev. and updated by John Trent.
    p. cm.
Includes bibliographical references.
ISBN 978-0-8499-4637-0 (trade paper)
1. Families—Religious life. 2. Child rearing—Religious aspects—Christianity. 3. Blessing and cursing. I. Smalley, Gary. II. Title.
BV4526.3.T74 2011
248.8'45—dc22   2011004971

Printed in the United States of America

23 24 25 26 27 LBC 5 4 3 2 1

Contents

CONTENTS

Part 3: Implementing the Blessing

Introduction

Every one of us, at some point in our lives, has at least one defining moment. Our life seemed forever stuck in uncertainty, confusion, or even in behaviors that were leading us along a path of destruction (or at least discomfort). But after that defining moment, our trajectory changed.

Something happened where we gained clarity and hope. We had a breakthrough and found purpose. The path steadied instead of being all uphill. The clouds blew away, and a positive path toward an optimistic future finally became clear. In my case, I found healing, and growth began anew.

For me, my defining moment came from the Blessing.

I don't share this lightly. I share this as the daughter of the man who came up with the idea for this book, as a child who grew up with parents who lived this out. They provided me with daily blessings and introduced me to a God who loved me. The Blessing wasn't just an idea in our family; it was, and still is, a critical part of our DNA.

However, as you will learn when you read this book, as powerful as the Blessing is, it is not a formula for perfection. It is not a guarantee that your children or grandchildren will never go through a season when they struggle. It's not a guarantee that they won't completely walk away from their faith or their family—as I did.

For five years, after I entered graduate school, my family had no idea where I was. All they knew was that the daughter they loved had cut off all contact, and something was terribly wrong. In reality, things were far worse than they ever could have imagined. What started with me walking away from my faith due to the Lord seeming intangible ended up with me eloping and experiencing unimaginable abuse in that relationship.

While you can read more about my story in this book, I'll summarize it here. I can honestly tell you that had it not been for the Lord rescuing me out of that situation, receiving the five elements of the Blessing growing up, and my parents' choice to bless me in healthy ways during my season of rebellion, I wouldn't be writing this today. I also wouldn't be doing ministry alongside my dad, helping a whole new generation of parents and children discover *the power of the Blessing*. I also wouldn't now have an incredible, godly, loving husband and two beautiful little boys.

For me, it really was the power of the Blessing that brought me home. Much like the prodigal son in the Bible, I finally reached a point when I figured my parents' anger and disapproval were better than where I was. So I returned to them after years of absence—and coincidently just hours after my ex-husband had arrived and vengefully shared with my family some of the horrible details of the past five years.

As I hung my head in their living room, and both confirmed and expanded on what my ex-husband had shared, I expected to hear a lecture. For them to yell or even to say, "Pack your bags." But what I got instead changed my life. It became my biggest defining moment.

After I was done sharing, my parents walked over to me and

put their hands on my shoulders. My dad said, "Kari, it's not about where you've been. It's about where you are going." And he and my mom each took a turn giving me their blessing.

Now, I want to be clear. Trust wasn't restored at that moment. All the hurt and brokenness weren't erased. And I still had a lot of personal healing to do. I still had to repair my relationship with my parents and my sister. But in that moment, I knew two crucial things: one, that my family still loved me and wanted a relationship with me, and, two, that I had their blessing and support to walk through the mess I had created.

Everything changed. I had permission to move forward. To heal. I didn't have to let the pain, sin, and mistakes of the past five years determine the rest of my life.

That truth unleashed me, and it will unleash you too. That kind of amazing, powerful, life-changing love, wrapped up in the biblical Blessing, frees you. And it's why the Blessing is so critical. It really does have the power to help someone who's lost find and regain their purpose. It has the power to help anyone, prodigal or saint, believe they really do have hope for the future, no matter what anyone else has ever said to them.

The Blessing opens a loved one's eyes to see their strengths, to understand how valuable they are to God, and to see great value in others. It allows them to know that the door of acceptance and welcome they've been knocking on all their lives really is fully open.

This truth is why your child—regardless of their age—needs your Blessing so much. This truth is why your spouse and whoever God has placed in your life-story needs your Blessing. Anyone who has grown up with a curse needs your Blessing.

In fact, the Blessing is something the Bible *commands* us to do. I love how this beautifully written translation reveals this truth in 1 Peter 3:8–12, where we're told,

"Bless—that's your job, to bless. You'll be a blessing and also get a blessing" (THE MESSAGE).

I believe the Bible calls us to bless not just because it's a good idea but because receiving the Blessing from God and from those most important people in your life—and choosing to give it to others—truly can change your life, just like it changed mine.

That's my prayer as you read this book, that you would choose to bless, that you would know that once you receive God's Blessing, even if you never received the Blessing growing up, you can break the worst of cycles. You can find God's power to bless your family and others. I pray that you'll understand how these five simple things matter so much on a relational and spiritual level. The Blessing really can become part of the DNA of *your* home.

Finally, know that every word of this book has been written by a family who has faced trials, imperfection, and brokenness. But we've also experienced the Blessing of a God whose love and Blessing is bigger than any challenge, relational divide, or circumstance. And we believe that is available for you and your family as well.

May you and those you love experience firsthand the power of the Blessing.

Kari Trent Stageberg

PART 1

WELCOME TO THE BLESSING

CHAPTER 1

The Importance of Asking Why and Discovering Who

Why does that deep ache of loneliness keep showing up in my life—even after my happiest moments or at the end of my biggest accomplishments? Why do I doubt whether I was really loved and cared for growing up, even though I didn't lack for any physical thing? Or perhaps you wonder, *Why do I try so hard to experience close, caring relationships and yet so often feel that the very thing I long for stays just out of reach?*

Have you ever been haunted by some version of that incredibly difficult question—*why?* In the incredibly powerful, biblical concept of the Blessing comes the answer for so many people about their deepest need from their most important earthly relationships, an answer to their *why?*

The Day I Found My *Why?* in the Word *Blessing*

It was several years ago that I experienced what was to me a God-inspired, profound discovery in regard to my own *why?* question. For me, it happened in a span of less than twenty-four hours, twelve of which I spent sitting with someone on suicide watch at a psychiatric hospital, where I was an intern.

My shift had ended. I remember walking out of the hospital that evening, wishing I could have been of more help to that very troubled young man and his *why?* I'd given him all the help and encouragement I could, but I didn't have a clear picture to show him. His *why?* had pushed him to the very brink of a life-and-death choice.

Little did I know that when I got home that night and opened my Bible to Genesis 27, I'd run right into the story of another man like the one I'd been sitting beside all day. Another person who was beyond heartbroken. In fact, we're told, "He cried with an exceedingly great and bitter cry, and said to his father, 'Bless me—me also, O my father!' . . . 'Have you not reserved a blessing for me?' . . . And Esau lifted up his voice and wept" (Genesis 27:34, 36, 38).

I had read about Jacob and Esau probably a hundred times. The story of one brother getting his father's blessing—and of the other being tricked out of it. But all of a sudden, as I sat in my study, it was like almighty God opened my eyes and the scales fell off. Now I had a name for that incredible longing I'd been listening to, that I'd seen in that hurting young man at the psychiatric hospital.

He had missed the Blessing. Whatever that was.

But without even knowing all that there was to Esau's cry right then, it was like a light turned on in my own mind and heart. That blessing, even though I didn't fully understand it, was something I knew I had longed for all my life with my own father, who had left our home when I was two months old. The story in Genesis 27 gave me the answer to that *why?* I was still struggling with in my own life. It painted a picture of my *why?* and gave me insight that could bring incredible help to many people I'd worked with. Not just at the hospital, but everyday people: friends and relatives; my own wife, who at that time had never gotten the Blessing from her father; and, certainly, those I worked with and counseled.

The thoughts *Why didn't you (or won't you) give me your blessing?* and even *Why is it so important to make sure we give others the Blessing?* sprang to my mind.

That very night, I started digging into Scripture to find the "return address" for Esau's crushing cry of emotional pain and separation—one that so many of us have echoed in our own lives.

The first verse that helped explain it to me wasn't far from that Genesis passage. The book of Deuteronomy records a time the Lord called the entire nation of Israel together and set before them something that was nothing less than a life-and-death choice—a choice that is set before us as well.

"I call heaven and earth to witness that I have set before you a choice. Life or death. The blessing or the curse. So choose life. You and your descendants" (Deuteronomy 30:19, author's paraphrase).

That's where I began to see the double-sided choice that the Lord himself had set before his people, just before they headed into the promised land. There was a choice: Life over death. Blessing over curse. One choice with two parts.

The Blessing originated in God giving us life and his blessing. But the deeper I dived into Scripture, the more I realized we also have a choice either to bless others or to withhold the Blessing from them! This choice begins with our children and our spouses, then extends to those around us. And in that choice to bless, amazingly, I found not only that huge *why?* answer but also how this concept of the Blessing helps answer the equally important question of *who?*

Discovering Who I Am Springs from the Blessing as Well

The question of *why?* helps us look back, deal with the hurt or loss, realize that very thing we've longed for all our lives, and finally understand that the choice someone (often a parent) made to bless us or withhold the blessing from us can impact our lives dramatically.

But the more I dug into the Blessing, the more it became clear how the five elements of the Blessing also help answer the equally important question of *who?*

Who am I?

Right at the heart of receiving the Blessing is a gift that helps us understand our identity: Who are we and who can we become? What are our strengths? Do I really have great value in God's eyes and in the eyes of crucial loved ones?

In the five elements of the Blessing, you'll see how appropriate touch and spoken words with attached high value can begin to give you a clearer picture of who you are—a picture of a special future and a deep sense of love and commitment that is absolutely necessary to understanding your purpose. The Blessing helps you answer the *who?* question as well.

The apostle Peter, one of Jesus' closest friends and disciples, wrote of Christ's suffering and how his love freed us, how it changes us and points our life in a new direction. At one point, he wrote, "Do not repay evil with evil or insult with insult. On the contrary, repay evil with blessing, because to this you were called so that you may inherit a blessing" (1 Peter 3:9 NIV).

In short, our calling is to be people of blessing.

Listen to the way Eugene Peterson in his eminently readable paraphrase, *The Message*, translates these same verses: "No retaliation. No sharp-tongued sarcasm. Instead, bless—that's your job, to bless. You'll be a blessing and also get a blessing."

Think about that for a moment.

That's your job: to bless.

You may have sworn it was to be a heavy-equipment operator or homemaker or policewoman or nurse practitioner or computer coder or teacher. No, your primary job is to bless. Not in your own strength. It begins and flows from God's blessing and loving you. As you unpack this biblical life-giving concept, the answers to why you're here and why you've needed the Blessing so much in your life can also help you answer the question, *Who am I?* In giving the Blessing, you can find your foundational identity and purpose. You can find your calling.

That's your job: to bless. For in blessing others, you'll see the Blessing change someone else's life. Even as it comes back from God himself and pours out all over you.

CHAPTER 2

The Lifelong Search for the Blessing

All of us long to be accepted by others. While we may say out loud, "I don't care what other people think about me," on the inside, we all yearn for intimacy and affection. Like it or not. Realize it or not. As our good friend Kenny Sanderfer often shares, we are all "created for connection."[1]

This yearning is especially true in our relationships with our parents. Gaining or missing out on parental approval has a tremendous effect on us, even if it has been years since we have had any contact with them. In fact, what happens in our relationship with our parents can greatly affect all our present and future relationships. While this may sound like an exaggeration, our offices have been filled with people struggling with this very issue.

We see it in the myriads who are driven toward workaholism as they search for the blessing they never received at home. Always hungry for acceptance and approval, they never feel satisfied that they are measuring up. Others get mired in withdrawal and apathy as they give up hope of ever truly being blessed. Unfortunately, this withdrawal can become so severe that it can lead to chronic depression and even suicide. For almost all children who miss out on their parents' blessing, at some level this lack of acceptance sets off a lifelong search.

The search for the Blessing is not just a modern-day phenomenon. It is actually centuries old. In fact, we can find a graphic picture of a person who missed out on his family's blessing in the Old Testament. Let's look now at a confused and angry man named Esau—the one who started my own adventure in learning about the Blessing. In so doing we will learn more about the Blessing and what it can mean to grow up with or without it.

"Bless Me—Me Also, O My Father!"

Esau was beside himself. *Could this really be happening?* he may have thought. Perhaps his mind went right back to the events of that day. Just hours before, his father, Isaac, had called him to his side and made a special request. If Esau, the older son, would go and bring in fresh game for a savory meal, Isaac's long-awaited blessing would be given to him.

What was this blessing that Esau had waited for over the years? For sons or daughters in biblical times, receiving their father's blessing was a momentous event. At a specific point in their lives, they could expect to feel a loving parent's touch and to hear words of encouragement, love, and acceptance—words that gave them a tremendous sense of being highly valued and that even pictured a special future for them.

We will see that some aspects of this Old Testament blessing were unique to that time. However, the *relationship elements* of this blessing are still applicable today. There was a Blessing given to the firstborn, and at times in Scripture we see a parent choose only one child to Bless. But know that each child could have been blessed! (See Genesis 49 where Jacob blessed each child.) Parents today can decide to build these elements of blessing into all their children's lives daily.

Esau's family, of course, had followed their culture's custom of waiting until a specific day to give the blessing, and the long-awaited day had come at last. Esau's time of blessing was supposed to begin as soon as he could catch and prepare the special meal.

With all the skill and abilities of an experienced hunter, Esau had gone about his work quickly and efficiently. In almost no time he had whipped up a delicious stew as only one familiar with the art of cooking in the field could do.

Esau had done just as he was told. Why, then, was Isaac acting so strangely? Esau had just entered his father's tent and greeted him:

> "Let my father arise and eat of his son's game, that your soul may bless me." And his father Isaac said to him, "Who are you?" So he said, "I am your son, your firstborn, Esau."
>
> Then Isaac trembled exceedingly, and said, "Who? Where is the one who hunted game and brought it to me? I ate all of it before you came, and I have blessed him— and indeed he shall be blessed."
>
> When Esau heard the words of his father, he cried with an exceedingly great and bitter cry, and said to his father, *"Bless me—me also, O my father!"* (Genesis 27:31– 34, italics added)

Little did Esau know that when his aged and nearly blind father called him to his side, another had been listening. Rebekah, the mother of Esau and his twin brother, Jacob, had also been in the tent. As soon as Esau went out into the fields to hunt fresh game, she had run to her favorite son, Jacob, with a cunning plan.

If they hurried, they could choose a young kid from the flock and prepare a savory meal. What's more, they could dress Jacob in his brother's clothing and put animal skins on him to simulate Esau's rough and hairy arms, hands, and neck.

Putting on Esau's clothes did not present a problem, but one thing they couldn't counterfeit was Esau's voice. That almost blew the whistle on them (v. 22). But even though Isaac was a little skeptical, their plan worked just as they had hoped it would. We read in Genesis 27:22–23, "So Jacob went near to Isaac his father. . . . And he did not recognize him, because his hands were hairy like his brother Esau's hands; so he blessed him." The blessing meant for the older son went to the younger.

Jacob should not have had to trick his way into receiving the blessing. God himself had told Isaac, regarding his twin sons, that the "older shall serve the younger" (Genesis 25:23). Yet Esau had grown up expecting the blessing to be his. No wonder he was devastated when he came back from hunting to find that an even more cunning hunter had stolen into his father's tent and taken what he thought would be his.

Was Esau crying over losing his inheritance? Absolutely not. As we will see later, the oldest son's inheritance was something that came with his birthright and entitled him to a double share in his father's wealth. Yet years before, Esau had already *sold* his birthright to his brother for a pot of red stew (Genesis 25:29–34).

No, Esau wasn't lamenting the fact that he lost the cattle and sheep—he had already despised that gift. What ripped at his heart was something much more personal: his father's blessing. In Old Testament times a father's blessing was irretrievable once it was given, so now Isaac's blessing was forever outside Esau's reach.

Filled with hurt, he cried out a *second* time, "'Do you have only one blessing, my father? Bless me, me as well, my father.' So Esau raised his voice and wept" (Genesis 27:38 NASB). In response to his pitiful cries, Esau did receive a blessing of sorts from his father (vv. 39–40), but it was not the words of high value and acceptance that he had longed to hear.

Can you feel the anguish in Esau's cry, "Bless me, me as well, O my father"? This same painful cry and unfulfilled longing are being echoed today by many people who are searching for their family's blessing, men and women whose parents, for whatever reason, have failed to bless them with words of love and acceptance. People with whom you rub shoulders every day. Perhaps even you.

The Importance of the Blessing

The hunger for genuine acceptance was a driving force in Esau's life—and it's a need that goes unmet in thousands of lives today. The family blessing provides that much-needed sense of personal acceptance. The Blessing also plays a part in protecting and even freeing people to develop intimate relationships. Perhaps most important, it lays the foundation for a genuine and fulfilling relationship with God that can survive even the rocky teen years, when many young people pull away from faith.

This is especially important today in a culture that offers many forms of counterfeit blessings to young people. Cult and gang leaders have mastered the elements of the Blessing. Providing a sense of family and offering (at least initially) the promise of personal attention, affection, and affirmation is an important drawing card for many of these groups. And our celebrity-saturated media falsely promises fulfillment and validation through money, fame, sex, and success.

Children who grow up without a sense of parental acceptance are especially susceptible to being drawn in by these counterfeit blessings. In fact, thousands are fooled every year, beckoned like hungry children to an imaginary dinner. But though the aroma of blessing may draw them to the table, after eating they are left hungrier than before.

Let's examine a little more closely the ways that being deprived of the Blessing can show itself later in life. Without the Blessing, children can become . . .

The Seekers

Seekers are people who are always searching for intimacy but are seldom able to tolerate it. These are the people who feel tremendous fulfillment in the thrill of courtship but may have difficulty sustaining a relationship of any kind, including marriage. Never sure of how acceptance feels, they are never satisfied with wearing it for too long. They may even struggle with believing in God's unchanging love for them because of the lack of permanence in the Blessing in their early lives.

The Shattered

These are the people whose lives are deeply troubled over the loss of their parents' love and acceptance. Fear, anxiety, depression, and emotional withdrawal can often be traced to missing out on the family blessing. This unhappy road can even lead a person to the terrifying cliffs of suicide, convinced they are destined to be a "cipher in the snow."

The Smotherers

Like two-thousand-pound sponges, these needy people react to missing their parents' blessing by sucking every bit of life and energy from a spouse, child, friend, or entire congregation. Their past has left them so empty emotionally that they eventually drain those around them of the desire to help or even listen. When this happens, unfortunately, the Smotherers understand only that they are being rejected. Deeply hurt once again, they never realize that they have brought this pain on themselves. They end up pushing away the very people they need so desperately.

The Angry

As long as people are angry with each other, they are emotionally chained together. Many adults, for instance, remain tightly linked to their parents because they are still furious over missing the Blessing. They have never forgiven or forgotten. As a result, the rattle and chafing of emotional chains distract them from intimacy in other relationships, and the weight of the iron links keeps them from moving forward in life.

The Detached

Quite a few children who have missed out on the Blessing use the old proverb "Once burned, twice shy" as a motto. Having lost the Blessing from an important person in their lives once, they spend a lifetime protecting themselves from it ever happening again. Keeping a spouse, children, or a close friend at arm's length, they protect themselves all right—at the expense of inviting loneliness to take up residence in their lives.

The Driven

In this category line up extreme perfectionists, workaholics, notoriously picky house cleaners, and generally demanding people who go after getting their blessing the old-fashioned way: they try to *earn it*. The thwarted need for affirmation and acceptance keeps these driven people tilting at a windmill named "accomplishment" in an illusory attempt to gain love and acceptance.

The Deluded

Like their driven counterparts, these people throw their time, energy, and material resources into the pursuit of anything they hope will fill that sense of emptiness inside. But instead of focusing on achievement, they look for social status, popularity, attention, and plenty of "toys." They never quite understand that the Blessing is a gift that cannot be bought. Only counterfeit blessings are for sale—usually at an exorbitant price—and they last only as long as the showroom shine on a new car. So these folks are constantly feeling the need to trade in one fake blessing for another.

The Seduced

Many people who have missed out on their parents' blessing look to fill their relationship needs in all the wrong places. As we mentioned in an earlier chapter, unmet needs for love and acceptance can tempt a person to sexual immorality, trying to meet legitimate needs in an illegitimate way. Substance abuse and other compulsive behaviors can also fall into this category. A drink, a pill, or a behavior is used to cover up the hurt from empty relationships in the past or present, and an addiction can easily result.[2] One study of compulsive gamblers (especially those struck with "lottery fever") found that more than 90 percent of the male subjects had "dismal childhoods, characterized by loneliness and rejection."[3]

If you are a parent, learning about the family blessing can help you provide your child(ren) with a protective tool. The best defense against imaginary acceptance is genuine acceptance. By providing genuine acceptance and affirmation at home, you can greatly reduce the likelihood that a child will seek those things in a gang hangout, a cult compound, or an immoral relationship.

Once again, let's affirm that we were all created for connection with others. That genuine acceptance and deep need for attachment we're born with radiates from the concept of the Blessing. However, the Blessing is not just an important tool for parents to use. The Blessing is also of critical importance for anyone who desires to draw close to another person in an intimate relationship. One of the most familiar verses in the Bible is Genesis 2:24: "For this reason a man shall leave his father and his mother, and be joined to his wife" (NASB).

Many books and other resources talk about the need to cleave—or attach firmly—to our spouses. However, very few talk about the tremendous need people also have to "leave" home. Perhaps this is because people have thought of leaving home as simply moving away physically.

In reality, leaving home has always meant much more than putting physical distance between our parents and ourselves. In the Old Testament, for example, the farthest most people would actually move away from their parents was across the campfire and into another tent! Leaving home carries with it not only the idea of physical separation but also of *emotional* separation.

The terrible fact is that most people who have missed out on their parents' blessing have great difficulty leaving home in this emotional sense. It may have been years since they have seen their parents, but unmet needs for personal acceptance can keep them emotionally chained to their parents, unable to genuinely cleave to another person in a lasting relationship.

It's one of the reasons many couples never get off the ground in terms of marital intimacy. You or a loved one may be facing this problem. Understanding the concept of the Blessing is crucial to defeating the problem and freeing people to build healthy relationships.

A Journey of Hope and Healing

In a world awash with insecurity, promoting soul-crushing isolation, and in search of acceptance, we need biblical anchors to hold on to—anchors like the Blessing.

The search for acceptance and heart-healing attachment that

so many people undertake often leads them to accept a cure that is worse than the problem itself. Many addictions, for instance, have their roots in the deep loneliness of growing up without a parent's blessing. In contrast, God's Word and his principles offer a dependable blueprint for constructing or reconstructing truly healthy relationships.

In the pages that follow you will discover more about the Blessing. You will explore the five crucial elements that make up the Blessing—and make it so powerful. You will also have a chance to look back and evaluate whether you received the Blessing as a child, how this childhood experience affects you and your family today, and how—if you missed out on the Blessing—you can find healing.

Most importantly, if you are a parent, you will discover how to make sure your children—toddlers to teens, and even those who are grown—receive the Blessing from you. In the process, you will be exposed to God's spiritual family blessing that is offered to each of his children.

If you are a teacher, discovering the Blessing can help you better understand your students. If you counsel others, it can provide a helpful framework for understanding many problems and offering practical solutions.[1] If you are involved in ministering to others,

---

1. Kari and I train Blessing and Attachment Life Coaches and "people helpers" who are looking for tools to build the Blessing into the lives of those they're working with. To find out more, go to StrongFamilies.com, and you'll find out how you can become a certified StrongFamilies coach. We also provide coaching for those who are struggling with any part of believing, receiving, giving, or living out the Blessing. We'd love to help you.

it can help you understand this crucial need every person has and provide resources for meeting that need.

Our prayer is, in the following pages, you will take the time and have the courage to journey into the past, a journey that can lead to hope and healing. Even more, we pray that you will be willing to look honestly at the present and apply what you discover.

These pages may end your lifelong search for acceptance or begin a new relationship with your children, your spouse, your parents, or a close friend. Our deepest desire is that this book will enrich your relationship with your heavenly Father as you learn more about the source of blessing that he is to each believer. All this as we take our first look at the life-changing concept called the Blessing.

CHAPTER 3

A Life-and-Death Choice

————

Just what is this blessing that seems to be so important? Does it really apply to us today, or was it just for Old Testament times? What are the elements that make up the Blessing? How can I know whether I have received it or if my children are experiencing it now?

These questions commonly surface as people are introduced to the Blessing. In answering them, we will discover five powerful relationship elements that the Old Testament blessing contains. The presence or absence of these elements can help us determine whether our home is—or our parents' home was—a place of blessing.

A study of the Blessing always begins in the context of parental acceptance. However, in studying the Blessing in the Scriptures, we found that its principles can be used in any intimate relationship.

Husbands can apply these principles in blessing their wives, and wives their husbands.

Friendships can be deepened and strengthened by including each element of the Blessing.

In short, do you love your child? Bless your child.

Do you love your spouse? Bless your spouse.

Do you love your mother or father? Bless your mother and father.

These key ingredients, when applied in a church family, can

bring warmth, healing, and hope to our brothers and sisters in Christ, many of whom never received an earthly blessing from their parents.

Perhaps the best place to begin our look at the benefits of giving or gaining the Blessing is to dig into the biblical ideas behind *blessing*—and the clear choice inherent in the word.

The Blessing and the Choice

Perhaps one of the clearest ways to begin to understand what the Blessing means is to look at an amazing choice God once laid before his people—the same choice that I believe is put in front of each of us today, a choice that is literally a matter of life and death. We introduced this thought and verse to you in the first chapter. Now let's dig deeper into this passage in the book of Deuteronomy, in the words that God spoke to Joshua:

> I call heaven and earth to witness against you today, that I have placed before you life and death, the blessing and the curse. So choose life in order that you may live, you and your descendants. (Deuteronomy 30:19 NASB)

The context in which these words were spoken can help us understand this idea of a choice. Joshua was the new leader of God's people. They had traveled all the way from Egypt and were finally ready to take their first steps into the promised land. Almighty God laid before them a path that he wanted them to follow—one that began with a crucial choice or, actually, two choices.

The first choice set before his people: life or death.

The second: blessing or curse.

Let's define our terms so we really understand how important these choices were to the Israelites and how they can affect our relationship with God and others today.

A Matter of Life and Death

The Hebrew word translated *life* in this passage carries with it the idea of movement.[1] In other words, things that are alive are things that are moving. Specifically, they're moving toward someone or something. So the first choice we have is to move toward God and toward others. When we do that, we add life to our relationships.

Think about a couple you know who have a great marriage. Almost always you will notice that they *take steps* to move toward each other—not just physically but emotionally. They choose to do things together. They choose to walk together toward a goal or interest or area they like.

Choosing life, then, means getting busy in moving toward the Lord or others. But there's the other side of this choice in the Deuteronomy passage as well. We can also choose death.

Interestingly, the word translated *death* also carries with it the concept of movement—in fact, its literal meaning is "to step away."[2] The idea is that death is stepping away from others, from life, from what we have built or shared with others.

Let's go back to our example of the couple. As a marriage counselor, time and again I've seen one spouse (or both) take a *step away* from the other when challenges come up. When they do this, something starts dying in their relationship. The more they move away from each other, the more problematic their marriage becomes.

So that's the life-or-death choice when it comes to relationships. At any given juncture we make the choice to move toward the other person, choosing life in that relationship, or to step away, choosing death.

To Bless or to Curse

To understand the second choice set before God's people in Joshua's time and in ours today—the blessing and the curse—let's take another look at the Hebrew words. For they also imply two very different paths we can choose to take with the Lord and with others.

The first idea contained in the Hebrew word for *bless* is that of "bowing the knee."[3] (Genesis 24:11 actually uses this word to describe a camel who must bend its knees so its master can get on.) Bowing before someone is a graphic picture of valuing that person.

Most Americans have never actually seen one person bow before another. But in biblical times (and in many cultures today), a person would bow before someone of great value—a king, a queen, a prophet, someone considered important and of high worth. When you bless someone, in other words, you are really saying, "I choose to treat you as someone incredibly valuable in my life." Of course, when we say, "Bless the Lord!" we're saying that as well:

"Lord, you are so incredibly valuable, you're worthy of our 'bowing the knee' before you."

Along with this first picture comes a second biblical word picture. The word for *bless* (and a similar word for *honor*) also carries the idea of adding weight or value to someone.[4] Literally, it's a picture of adding coins to a scale. In biblical times, you didn't just hand someone a coin with a specific denomination stamped on it as we do today. In Old Testament times, a coin might carry an inscription or even a picture of a ruler or someone of great value. But the way you determined how much it was worth was to put it on a scale. The greater the weight, the higher the value.

Let's put those two pictures together now to gain a sharper focus on what it means to bless someone. You are basically saying, "You are of such great value to me, I choose to add to your life." And as you'll soon see, there are five specific actions you can take (the five elements of the Blessing) to do just that for another person.

But what about the opposite choice—the curse? In understanding the word picture behind this word, I think you'll see it's a choice that many continue to make today. In fact, any of us can make the choice to curse others instead of blessing them. We do that when we subtract the things that would add life for the other person.

The word for *curse* in this passage literally means a "trickle" or "muddy stream" caused by a dam or obstruction upstream.[5] For Joshua's people, living in desert lands, cutting off water meant cutting off life itself. So do you get the terrible word picture here? When we curse someone, we are choosing to "dam up the stream" on life-giving actions and words that could flow down to that person.

Think of a desert dweller in biblical times who walks for miles to find a life-giving stream, only to get there and find a muddy trickle because someone dammed up the brook. But now picture someone choosing to break down the dam—choosing to add what was missing, bringing life where there had been death.

A beautiful example of this is found in John 4, when Jesus sat down with the woman at the well. This woman was more or less an outcast in her town—married five times, now living out of wedlock with a sixth man. She came to draw water in the heat of the day, when no one else was around, probably avoiding the other women in the village. And she was a Samaritan, looked down on by all Jews. So many aspects of her life acted to dam up the flow of blessings in her life—by that definition, she was cursed.

But do you remember what Jesus offered this woman? He offered her "living water" (John 4:10–15). And that's because God is the one who can break down all the things in our lives that curse us, slowing the flow of what we need to a trickle. It is he who blesses us with a flow of living water.

In Deuteronomy 23:5, God put it this way: "The LORD your God would not listen to Balaam [someone hired by the Hebrews' enemies to curse them], but the LORD your God turned the curse into a blessing for you, because the LORD your God loves you."

That's God's choice, of course, but the choice to bless or curse others is ours as well. We are told in the book of Proverbs that "death and life are in the power of the tongue" (Proverbs 18:21). So it is with the blessing, and so it is in a terribly negative way when we choose the curse.

It's our choice then—yours and mine.

Will we choose life and move toward others, or choose death and step away?

Will we choose to bless our loved ones and the Lord by bowing our knees and weighing our scales in their favor—opening our lives to God's blessing in the process? Or will we choose to curse them by blocking the flow of good things in our own lives and others' lives?

If you are ready to choose life and blessing, let's be even more specific about those five elements of the Blessing that biblical parents gave and that children today—children of all ages—long for as well. Mark well each element of the blessing as it applies to your own life. Did you receive each of the elements? Are you giving it to your loved ones and others? Are you making that life-and-death choice?

PART 2

THE ELEMENTS OF THE BLESSING

CHAPTER 4

The First Element: Appropriate
Meaningful Touch

Holding and hugging a four-year-old is permissible in most homes. But what about the need a fourteen-year-old has to be meaningfully touched by his mother or father (even if the teenager outwardly cringes every time they are hugged)? What about a thirty-four-year-old—or a spouse or close friend?

We all need appropriate meaningful touch and suffer when we are deprived of it. However, children are particularly affected by the absence of touch. Sometimes it can so affect a child that they spend a lifetime reaching out for arms that will never embrace them.

In the Old Testament, touch played an important part in the bestowal of the family blessing. When Isaac blessed Jacob, an embrace and a kiss were involved. We read, "Then his father Isaac said to him, 'Please come close and kiss me, my son'" (Genesis 27:26 NASB).

The Hebrew word for "come close" is very descriptive. It is used of armies drawn together in battle. It is even used to picture the overlapping scales on a crocodile's skin.[1] It may have been a while since you last saw a battle or a crocodile, but these word pictures still call up in our minds a picture of a very close connection.

Isaac wasn't asking his son to give him an "Aunt Ethel hug." (Remember Aunt Ethel—the one who pinched your cheek, then bent over and repeatedly patted you on the back when she hugged you?) Free from the current taboos our culture sets on a man embracing his son, Isaac was calling Jacob close to give him a bear hug.

For fathers in North America, there is a strong correlation between the age of a son and whether his father will touch him.[2] Yet Isaac's grown son was at least *forty years old* when he said, "Come close and kiss me, my son."[3]

Children of all ages need appropriate meaningful touch, particularly from a father. Studies have showed that mothers touch their children in more nurturing ways and fathers in more playful ways. But when the children were interviewed, they perceived their fathers' touch as more nurturing—perhaps because it didn't happen as often.[4]

Our need for appropriate meaningful touch does not go away when we enter grade school. Isaac didn't set up barriers around the need to be touched. He was a model that parents, husbands and wives, and even friends at church need to follow in giving the Blessing.

The Power of Appropriate Meaningful Touch

Toward the end of the book of Genesis, we find another clear example of including appropriate meaningful touch in bestowing the Blessing. This time the blessing involved a grandfather who wanted to make sure his grandchildren received this special gift of personal experience. Let's look in on the "touching" scene:

> Joseph said to his father, "They are my sons, whom God has given me in this place."
>
> And he said, "Please bring them to me, and I will bless them." Now the eyes of Israel were dim with age, so that he could not see. Then Joseph brought them near him, and he kissed them and embraced them. . . .
>
> Then Israel stretched out his right hand and laid it on Ephraim's head . . . and his left hand on Manasseh's head. (Genesis 48:9–10, 14)

Jacob (whose name had been changed to Israel) not only kissed his grandchildren and held them close but also placed his hands on each grandson's head.[5] This practice of laying on of hands was an important part of many of the religious rituals for the biblical patriarchs.

There are at least two important reasons why placing our hands on someone as a part of the Blessing is so special. First, there is a symbolic meaning attached to touching, and second, there are tremendous physical benefits to the laying on of hands.

The symbolic picture of the laying on of hands was important. This touch presented a graphic picture of transferring power or blessing from one person to another.[6] For example, in the book of Leviticus, Aaron was instructed to use this practice in his priestly duties. On the Day of Atonement, he was to place his hands on the head of a goat that was then sent into the wilderness. This picture is of Aaron symbolically transferring the sins of Israel onto that animal. (It is also a prophetic picture of how Christ, like that spotless animal, would take on our sins at the cross.) In another example, Elijah passed along his role as God's prophet to Elisha by the laying on of hands.

We realize that today there is so much brokenness from trauma and inappropriate touch. Everyone has learned during the pandemic to stand back from others at least six feet. And school children—who need appropriate touch so much—were isolated and never touched or patted on the shoulder. A cascade of studies is now linking this isolation with the emotional hurt and deepening loneliness many children and young adults are dealing with.

But the symbolic meaning of touch is still powerful. While we may not be consciously aware of it, the way we touch can carry tremendous symbolic meaning.

A young woman holding hands with a new boyfriend can signal "I'm taken" to other would-be suitors. Two businesspeople shaking hands can signify that an important deal has been completed. A minister at a wedding says to a couple, "If you then have freely and lawfully chosen one another as husband and wife, please *join hands* as you repeat these vows."

While important symbolism accompanies our touch, it is not the only reason God made it a part of the Blessing. Appropriate meaningful touch also communicates blessing on a very basic, physical level. For one thing, over one-third of our five million touch receptors are centered in our hands![7]

Interestingly enough, the act of laying on of hands, associated with the biblical blessing, has more recently become the focus of a great deal of secular interest and research. Dr. Dolores Krieger, a professor of nursing at New York University, has done numerous studies on the effects of laying on of hands. What she found is that both the toucher and the one being touched receive a psychological benefit from this practice.[8]

How is that possible? Inside our bodies is hemoglobin, the pigment of the red blood cells, which carries oxygen to the tissues. Repeatedly, Dr. Krieger has found that hemoglobin levels in *both* people's bloodstreams go up during the act of laying on of hands. As hemoglobin levels are invigorated, body tissues receive more oxygen. This increase in oxygen energizes a person and can even aid in the regenerative process if they are ill.

We are sure that Ephraim and Manasseh were not thinking, *Wow, our hemoglobin levels are going up!* when their grandfather laid his hands on them. However, one of the things that certainly stayed with them as they looked back on their day of blessing was the old patriarch's gentle touch.

Hugs and kisses were also a part of appropriate meaningful touching pictured in the Scriptures. Let's look further at the physical benefits of touching and the deep emotional needs that can be met by this first element of the family blessing.

How would you like to lower your husband's or wife's blood pressure? Protect your grade-school child from being involved in an immoral relationship later in life? Even add up to two years to your own life? (Almost sounds like an insurance commercial, doesn't it?) Actually, these are all findings in studies on the incredible power to bless found in appropriate meaningful touching.

More Reasons Why Appropriate Meaningful Touch Blesses Us Physically

Every day, researchers are discovering more and more information about the importance of touch. If we are serious about being a source of blessing to others, we must consider putting these important points into practice. As we saw in the studies of the laying on of hands, a number of physical changes take place when we reach out and touch.

A study at UCLA found, for example, that men and women need eight to ten meaningful touches a day just to maintain emotional and physical health. Gary shared this information once at a marriage seminar. And as he was talking, he noticed a man in the second row reach over and begin patting his wife on the shoulder and counting, "One, two, three . . ." That is *not* what the study meant by meaningful touch.[9]

The UCLA researchers defined meaningful touch as a gentle touch, stroke, kiss, or hug given by significant people in our lives (a husband or wife, parent, close friend, and so on). They even estimated that if some type-A, driven men would hug their wives several times each day, they could increase their life spans by almost two years (not to mention the way it would improve their marriages)!

Obviously, we can physically bless those around us (and even ourselves) with appropriate meaningful touch. But touching does much more than that.

Do you have a newborn in your home? Newborns make

tremendous gains if provided with appropriate meaningful touch—and may be at risk if they aren't.

Researchers at the University of Miami Medical School's Touch Research Institute began giving premature babies forty-five-minute massages each day. Within ten days, the massaged babies showed 47 percent greater weight gain than those children who were not regularly touched.[10] A second study showed that the actual bone growth of young children who had been deprived of parental touching was half that of children who received adequate physical attention.[11]

And in groundbreaking studies, Dr. Schanberg and Dr. Butler at Duke University Medical School found that without maternal touch, rat pups do not produce a type of protein crucial to their growth and development. When these rat pups were separated and unable to feel their mother's touch, they responded by slowly shutting down the production of an enzyme crucial to the development of major organs. As soon as the pups were reunited with their mother, however, enzyme production returned to normal.[12]

Even the smallest act of touch can help a child who is unable to move. One group of physically handicapped children was placed on a smooth surface (like smooth Naugahyde) and a second group on a highly textured surface (like a rubber floor mat). EMG studies showed marked differences between the two groups, including increases in muscle tone simply from placing children on a textured surface.[13]

You can't get away from it. Overwhelming evidence shows that physical touch benefits and blesses children (and animals). But how about adults?

Are your parents getting up in years? Appropriate meaningful touch can be an important part of maintaining health and a positive attitude in older persons. In a practice that has become commonplace now, residents in nursing homes were brought together with pets from a neighboring animal shelter. At first it was thought to be just a good recreational activity. Upon further study, more significant results began to surface. Those residents who had a pet to touch and hold not only lived longer than those without a pet but also had a more positive attitude about life![14]

Elderly patients with more serious problems have also demonstrated a number of tremendous benefits from regular, appropriate meaningful touch. For those suffering from dementia, a regimen of regular meaningful touch significantly increased their nutritional intake, helping them gain needed weight.[15] In addition, with Alzheimer's patients, physical touch decreased strange movements and repetitious mannerisms such as picking up objects again and again.[16]

Appropriate Meaningful Touch
Blesses Our Relationships

An interesting study done at Purdue University demonstrates how important touch is in determining how we view someone else. Librarians at the school were asked by researchers to alternately touch and not touch the hands of students as they handed back their library cards. The experimenters then interviewed the students. Do you know what they found? You guessed it. Those who had been touched reported far greater positive feelings about both the library and the librarian than those who were not touched.[17]

A doctor I know, a noted neurosurgeon, did his own study on the effects of brief times of touch. With half his patients in the hospital, he would sit on their beds and touch them on the arm or leg when he came in to see how they were doing. With his remaining patients, he would simply stand near the bed to conduct his interview of how they were feeling.

Before the patients went home from the hospital, the nurses gave each patient a short questionnaire evaluating the treatment they received. They were especially asked to comment on the amount of time they felt the doctor had spent with them. While in actuality he had spent the same amount of time in each patient's room, those people he had come near and touched felt he had been in their room nearly twice as long as those he had not touched.

Other studies have shown similar results in very different circumstances. For example, airline passengers who were touched "accidentally" by flight attendants on a long-distance flight rated those attendants as more qualified, the airline as more professional, and the plane trip *safer* than those who were not touched.[18]

Come on, Trent, you may be thinking. *Do you really mean that a touch lasting a few seconds or less can help me build better relationships?* Actually, we hope you can touch your loved ones much more than that, but even small acts of touch can indeed leave a lasting impression.

Touching a child on the shoulder when they walk in front of you, holding hands with your spouse while you wait in line, stopping for a moment to ruffle someone's hair—all these small acts can change how you are viewed by others and even how they view themselves. A ten-minute bear hug is not the only way to give another person the Blessing. At times, the *smallest* act of touch can be a vehicle for communicating love and personal acceptance.

Parents, in particular, need to know that neglecting to meaningfully touch their children starves them of genuine acceptance—so much so that it can drive them into the arms of someone else who is all too willing to touch them. Analyzing why some young people are drawn to cults, one author writes, "Cults and related movements offer a new family. They provide the follower with new people to worry about him, to offer him advice, to cry with him, and importantly, to hold him and touch him. Those can be unbeatable attractions."[19]

They certainly can, especially if appropriate meaningful touch has not been a part of the blessing a child receives. Even if a child is not lured into a cult to make up for years of touch deprivation, they can be drawn into the arms of an immoral relationship.

Women who repeatedly have unwanted pregnancies have told researchers that their sexual activity is merely a way of satisfying yearnings to be touched and held. Dr. Marc Hollender, a noted psychiatrist, interviewed scores of women who have had three or more unwanted pregnancies. Overwhelmingly, these women said that they were "consciously aware that sexual activity was a price to be paid for being cuddled and held." Touching before intercourse was more pleasurable than intercourse itself, "which was merely something to be tolerated."[20]

Touch from both a mother and father is important. If you are a single parent, your choice to provide appropriate touch is hugely important as well. Appropriate meaningful touching can protect a child from looking to meet this need in all the wrong places.

If we ignore the physical and emotional needs our children, spouse, or close friends have for appropriate meaningful touch, we deny them an important part of the Blessing. What's more, we shatter a biblical guideline that our Lord Jesus himself set in blessing others.

Jesus and the Blessing of Appropriate Meaningful Touch

Jesus was a model of someone who communicated the Blessing to others. In fact, his blessing of children in the Gospels parallels the important elements of the family blessing, including appropriate meaningful touch. Let's look at Mark's account of that blessing.

> Then they brought little children to Him, that He might touch them; but the disciples rebuked those who brought them. But when Jesus saw it, He was greatly displeased and said to them, "Let the little children come to Me, and do not forbid them; for of such is the kingdom of God." . . . And He took them up in His arms, laid His hands on them, and blessed them. (Mark 10:13–14, 16)

Appropriate meaningful touching was certainly a part of Christ's blessing as Mark described it. Mobbed by onlookers and protected by his disciples, Jesus could have easily waved to the children from a distance or just ignored them altogether. But he did neither. Jesus would not even settle for the politicians' "chuck under the chin" routine; rather, he "took them up in His arms, laid His hands on them, and blessed them."

In this moment, Jesus was not simply communicating a spiritual lesson to the crowds. He could have done that by simply placing one child in the center of the group as he did on another occasion (Matthew 18:2). Here, Jesus was demonstrating his knowledge of the genuine importance of touch to a child.

For children, things become real when they are touched. Have you ever been to Disneyland and seen the look on little ones' faces when they come face-to-face with a person dressed like Goofy or Donald Duck? Even if they are initially fearful, soon they will want to reach out and touch the Disney character. This same principle allows children to stand in line for hours to see Santa Claus—the same children who normally can't stand still for five minutes.

Jesus was a master of communicating love and personal acceptance. He did so when he blessed and held these little children. But another time his sensitivity to the importance of touch played itself out more dramatically, when Jesus chose to touch a man who was barred by law from ever touching anyone again:

And a man with leprosy came to Jesus, imploring Him and kneeling down, and saying to Him, "If You are willing, You can make me clean." Moved with compassion, *Jesus reached out His hand and touched him*, and said to him, "I am willing; be cleansed." And immediately the leprosy left him, and he was cleansed. (Mark 1:40–42 NASB, italics added)

In Jesus' day, touching a leper was unthinkable. Fear banished them from society, and people would not get within a stone's throw of them. In fact, they would throw stones at them if they did come close.[21] A parallel passage in Luke tells us that this man was "covered with leprosy" (Luke 5:12 NASB). With their open sores covered by dirty bandages, lepers were the last people anyone would want to touch. Yet the first thing Christ did when he met this man, even before he spoke to him, was to reach out his hand and *touch* him.

Can you imagine what that scene must have looked like? Think how this man must have longed for someone to touch him, not throw stones at him to drive him away. And remember, Jesus could have healed him first and then touched him. But recognizing the leper's deepest need, Jesus stretched out his hand even before he spoke words of physical and spiritual healing.

Wherever you live across the United States, you may not come from a warm, affectionate background. Sociologist Sidney Jourard studied the touch behavior of pairs of people in coffee shops around the world. The difference between cultures was staggering. In San Juan, Puerto Rico, people touched on average 180 times per hour. In Paris, France, it was 110 times per hour. In Gainesville, Florida, 2 times per hour. And in London, England, *0* times per hour.[22]

We Americans aren't known as a country of huggers, and with all the media reports of child abuse and sexual misconduct, we have backed away from touch even more. We need to realize, however, that avoiding healthy, appropriate meaningful touch sacrifices physical and emotional health in our lives and the lives of our loved ones.

If we want to be people who give the Blessing to others, one thing is clear. Just like Isaac, Jacob, and Jesus, we must include appropriate meaningful touch in our contacts with loved ones. This element of the Blessing can lay the groundwork for the second key aspect of the Blessing—a message that is put into words.

CHAPTER 5

The Second Element: A Spoken or Written Message

———

Words have the incredible power to build us up or tear us down emotionally. This is particularly true when it comes to giving or gaining family approval. Many people can clearly remember words of praise their parents spoke years ago. Others can remember negative words they heard—and what their parents were wearing when they spoke them!

We should not be surprised, then, that the family blessing hinges on being a *verbalized* message. Abraham *spoke* a blessing to Isaac. Isaac *spoke* it to his son Jacob. Jacob *spoke* it to each of his twelve sons and to two of his grandchildren. Esau was so excited when he was called in to receive his blessing because, after years of waiting, he would finally *hear* the blessing. Later, the apostle Paul wrote eloquent words of blessing to growing churches all over the Roman Empire.

In the Scriptures, a blessing is not a blessing unless it is put into words and actually communicated.

The Power of Words

If you are a parent, your children desperately need to receive *words* of blessing from you. If you are married, your wife or husband needs to receive *words* of love and acceptance on a regular basis. This very week with a friend, a coworker, or someone at your church, you will rub shoulders with someone who needs to receive *words* of encouragement.

Throughout the Scriptures, we find a keen recognition of the power and importance of words. In the very beginning, God spoke and the world came into being (Genesis 1:3). When he sent us his Son to communicate his love and complete his plan of salvation, it was his *Word* that "became flesh and dwelt among us" (John 1:14). God has always been a God who communicates his blessing through words.

In the book of James, three word pictures grab our attention and point out the power and importance of words. All three illustrate the ability the tongue (the primary conveyer of words) has to build up or break down relationships, the ability to bless or to curse.

First, the tongue is pictured as a "bit" used to direct a horse (see James 3:3). If you control a horse's mouth by means of a small bit, the entire animal will move in the direction you choose. (You might have ridden a few horses that seem to be exceptions, but the general rule is certainly true.) The second picture illustrates this same principle in a different way. Here a "small rudder" is used to turn a great ship (3:4). These analogies point out the way words can direct and control a person or a relationship.

Parents, spouses, or friends can use this power of the tongue for good. They can steer a child away from trouble or provide guidance to a friend who is making an important decision. They can minister words of encouragement or lift up words of praise. But this power can also be misused, sometimes with tragic results.

That is what the third word picture shows us. It illustrates all too clearly that words can burn deeply into a person's life, often setting the course that person's future will take. Listen to the awesome power a verbalized message can have: "The tongue is a small part of the body, and yet it boasts of great things. See how great a forest is set aflame by such a small fire! And the tongue is a fire, the very world of unrighteousness . . . and sets on fire the *course of our life*" (James 3:5–6 NASB, italics added). Just like a forest fire, what we say to others can burn deeply into their hearts.

Perhaps you still stumble over hurtful words your parents, spouse, or a close friend once conveyed to you (or negative words you have communicated to yourself), words that come to memory time and again and point you in a direction in life you don't want to go. If so, don't lose hope. As you learn more about the Blessing, you can begin to receive and give words that can lead to a new course of life.

Each of us should be keenly aware of the power of our words. We should also be aware of how powerful the *absence* of such words can be.

Today's Most Common Choice: "I'll Tell Them Tomorrow"

Negative words have the power to shatter children emotionally rather than shape them positively. But that is not the most common choice of parents. Most parents genuinely love their children and want the best for them. However, when it comes to sharing words of love and acceptance—words of blessing—they are up against an even more formidable foe than the temptation to communicate negative words.

A thief is loose in many homes today who masquerades as

fulfillment, *accomplishment*, and *success*. This thief steals the precious gift of genuine acceptance from our children and leaves confusion and emptiness in its place. The villain's real name is *overactivity*, and it can keep parents so busy that the Blessing is never shared, even with parents who dearly love their children; as one woman said, "Who has the time to stop and *tell* them?"

In many homes today both parents are working overtime, and a family night makes an appearance about as often as Halley's Comet. The result is instead of Dad and Mom taking the time to communicate words of blessing, a babysitter named *silence* is left to mold a child's self-perception. Life is so hectic that, for many parents, that "just right" time to share a verbal blessing never quite comes around. What is the result?

A father tries to corner his son to communicate "how he feels about him" before he goes away to college, but now his son is too busy to listen.

A mother tries to communicate words of blessing to her daughter in the bride's room just before the wedding, but the photographer has to take her away to get that perfect shot.

Words of blessing should start in the delivery room and continue throughout life. Yet the "lack of time" and the thief's motto, "I'll have time to tell them tomorrow," rob the children of a needed blessing today.

"Oh, it's not that big a deal," you may say. "They know I love them and that they're special without my having to say it." Really? We wish that explanation worked with many of the people we counsel. To them, their parents' silence has communicated something far different from love and acceptance.

Words Matter

Are words or their absence *really* that powerful? Solomon thought so. His words are like ice water in our faces, shocking us into reality: "Death and life are in the power of the tongue" (Proverbs 18:21).

If we struggle with communicating words of love and acceptance to our families or friends, another proverb should encourage us. Again, it is Solomon writing: "Do not withhold good from those to whom it is due, when it is in the power of your hand to do so. Do not say . . . 'Go, and come back, and tomorrow I will give it,' when you have it with you" (Proverbs 3:27–28).

If we can open our mouths to talk, we have the ability to communicate the Blessing through spoken words. As we will see, writing out words of blessing can be equally powerful, especially when spoken words aren't possible. In fact, written words of blessing have their own special advantage in that they can be composed more carefully and deliberately and can be kept and reread.

Why Is It So Hard to Express Words of Blessing?

If words of love and acceptance are so important, why are they offered so infrequently? Here are a few reasons we have gathered from people we have counseled:

- "I don't want to inflate my child's ego."
- "I'm afraid if I praise them, they'll take advantage of me and won't finish their work."

- "Communication is too much like work. I work all day, then she expects me to work all night talking to her."
- "I just don't know what to say."
- "They know I love them without my having to say it."
- "If I get started, I'll have to make a habit of it."
- "If I don't say it perfectly, it will just make things worse, or it won't really matter."

Then there's our personal favorite:

- "Telling children their good points is like putting on perfume. A little is okay, but put on too much, and it stinks."

As far as we are concerned, it's that statement that stinks. And none of those explanations come anywhere close to the real reason many people hesitate to bless their children or others with words of love and acceptance.

The real reason most people withhold this part of the Blessing is that their parents never gave it to them. Both praise and criticism seem to trickle down through generations. That means if you never heard words of love and acceptance, you could expect to struggle with sharing them yourself. Why? It's as if your family had a rule that loving words were best left unsaid, and you may find it very difficult to break this rule.

Every family operates by certain rules, spoken or unspoken, that prescribe "the way our family does things." Some families have a rule that "people who know anything about anything" open Christmas presents on Christmas *morning*. Other families follow the rule that "truly civilized people" open Christmas presents on Christmas *Eve*. Conflicting family rules often meet in a marriage. Many an argument has gone fifteen rounds to see whose family rule will win out in a new marriage.

Families set all kinds of rules: what we will eat in this family and what we won't eat. What television programs we can watch and which are dull or off-limits. What is safe to talk about and what subjects should never be brought up. Whom we invite over to the house and who doesn't get an invitation.

In some cases family rules can be very helpful. For example, families can adopt biblical rules like not letting the sun go down on anger and being kind one to another. Another way of setting positive family rules is by using contracts that can help build communication and encourage children.[1] These types of family guidelines can be safely passed down from generation to generation.

But not all family rules are worth retaining. In fact, some can devastate a family. Like words cast in steel, a destructive family rule can hammer away at a family from parent to son or daughter. The process will continue from generation to generation until at last someone breaks this painful pattern.

Putting Words of Blessing into Practice

We put words of blessing into practice in our homes and relationships by deciding to speak up rather than clam up. Good intentions aside, good words are needed to bestow the Blessing on a child, spouse, or friend.

Note that we are not simply saying, "*Talk more* to your children or others." While talking is normally a good idea, sometimes if you don't know how to communicate in a positive way, you can say less by saying more. As we will see in the next chapter, it is not just *any* words but words of high value that attach themselves to a person and communicate the Blessing. These are the kinds of words you often hear in the final hours before a family reunion ends.

Almost all of us have had the opportunity to attend a family reunion. A common phenomenon at these gatherings is that during the first two days, everyone is busy talking up a storm about this recipe, that football team, this book they've read, or that movie to attend. But something happens on the last afternoon of the reunion. Suddenly, with only an hour left before family members say their goodbyes, meaningful words will begin to be spoken.

But what do you say? The Blessing was always a tremendous time for a parent or loved one to use their words to "picture" or point out strengths they see in that loved one. For example, a brother will say in private to his sister, "I know things are really tough right now in your marriage. But you're strong and caring and loving. I'm praying things will work for you." Or an aunt will say to her niece, "You've always made me proud. I know school is hard, but you are so persistent. All your life I've seen that in you. And I know you can do it now. I believe in you." Or a daughter will say to a parent, "Look around you, Mom. We didn't turn out half bad, did we? We have you and Dad to thank."

So often, we seem to need the pressure of time before we say things closest to our hearts. But when it comes to your children, your spouse, your close friends, and even your parents, it may be later than you think. In some relationships, it is already late afternoon in your opportunity to talk to those you love.

Ask any family who has watched a son or daughter go off to war. We hang on to words from them. We long to get our words of love and prayers for their safety to them. Words carry the Blessing, and in the next chapter, you can learn about the kind of words—words of high value—that can especially bless people.

But don't delay. Time passes so quickly. Please don't let that important person leave your life without receiving the second element of the Blessing—the spoken (or written) word.

CHAPTER 6

The Third Element:
Attaching High Value

———

What do we mean by "high value"? Let's look at the word *value* to see the part it plays in the Blessing.

To value something means to attach great importance to it. This is at the very heart of the concept of blessing. As we saw earlier, the root word for *blessing* carries the dual meaning of "bow the knee" and to "add value." In relationship to God, the word came to mean "to adore with bended knees."[1] Bowing before someone is a graphic picture of valuing that person.

Notice the important principle here: anytime we bless someone, we are attaching a high value to them. It bears repeating that when we bless someone, we are deciding—choosing—to hold on to the fact that they are of high value. That is what the psalmist was telling us in Psalm 103:1 when he said, "Bless the LORD, O my soul; and all that is within me, bless His holy name!" When we "bless the Lord," we are actually recognizing God's intrinsic worth and attaching high value to him. We are saying that he is worthy of our bowing the knee to him.[2]

In the Scriptures we are often called on to bless or value the Lord, but the Scriptures also give many examples of humans blessing other humans (Deuteronomy 33:1–2; Joshua 14:13; 2 Samuel

6:18; and others). When they did so, each was attaching high value to the person he was blessing, recognizing them as a very special individual.

This is exactly what the patriarchs in the Old Testament were doing when they extended the family blessing to their children—attaching a high value to them. We do the same when we bless our children, spouses, or friends. This concept of valuing another person is so important that we believe it can be found at the heart of every healthy relationship.

You'll hear time and again the term *attachment* and even *attachment theory*, which is being promoted everywhere. But long before clinical studies were released about the need for connection, the idea of attachment was at the very foundation of the Blessing. For when God blesses us—or we bless others—we're saying, "I'd choose you!" "You have great value to me!" It's recognition that we're incredibly important to someone. That someone is "crazy about us." That God is crazy about us! That's why every person needs the Blessing from God and from a significant loved one and why the Blessing is such a huge key to people feeling truly loved and secure about themselves.

We Communicate High
Value with Our Eyes

Our good friend and neuroscientist Dr. Jim Wilder teaches people about the incredible need for joy and attachment in healthy brain development. Amazingly, long before brain science weighed in, the Blessing in Scripture communicated both. This idea of our brains needing joy and attachment comes from the way our brain works.

Each person constantly scans the world, not just to see if they're safe but also to see if there is someone they're connected with. It's like asking the questions, *Is there someone there who loves me? Who sees me? Who looks at me as though I have high value?* That's what brings us joy, safety, love, and emotional health.[1]

Dr. Wilder shared this with me: "What we've discovered is that love moves at the speed of joy. Meaning when we see someone who looks at us with love. That look goes right to our hearts. And that begins with using our eyes to do what it says in Scripture: 'Bright eyes make the heart glad' (Proverbs 15:30)."

Love Moves at the Speed of a Tired Mom's Look

I can remember as a child *knowing* that I was valuable. As I look back, in large part, it was because of what happened constantly when I was young. I saw it almost every day when my single-parent mother would pull into the driveway of our home after a long day at work.

As young kids we knew the time when she would arrive home. Often we'd all three already be at the window. The instant

---

1. Jim Wilder and Michel Hendricks, *The Other Half of Church: Christian Community, Brain Science, and Overcoming Spiritual Stagnation* (Chicago: Moody Publishers, 2020), 18–19.

we saw her car arrive, my two brothers and I would race one another outside, erupting out of the back door. I later realized our actions were because we were about to be met with that look of joy and love.

I'm not sure if my mom needed a moment to prepare herself before getting overtaken by her three sons. But every time she got out of her beat-up Ford Falcon, what we saw wasn't her exhaustion or worry. It was a face totally lit up with love. Her eyes. That smile. That look on her face as we ran to her revealed she was crazy about each of us.

That's where high value begins. *In short, every child, in every home, deserves to know that at least one person in their life is crazy about them.* And a beginning point for doing just that is how we look at them.

When we look at our children like they indeed have high value, that look of love races right to their hearts and minds. Imagine wandering around a party where you don't know anyone. After a while, it can become uncomfortable not to feel like you've connected with anyone. But then, all of a sudden, there's that one person you know. And they not only recognize you but their eyes are lit up. They move toward you in warmth and friendship. That's when you know you belong.

Yes, it's okay to feel tired and not to walk around constantly with your eyes wide open with love and attachment on your face. But during those key times when you first see someone, when a child needs encouragement, or when somebody just needs to know they're valuable, high value can start with your eyes.

Those are the times when your words are incredibly important.

Powerful "word pictures" were used often in Scripture whenever a Blessing was given. These words highlighted the strength God has put inside a child or loved one we want to bless.

Words of High Value in Old Testament Homes

In the Old Testament, spoken words that attach high value to a child are like shining threads of love and value running through the fabric of a blessing. Remember Isaac's word picture, "Surely, the smell of my son is like the smell of a field which the LORD has blessed" (Genesis 27:27)? But Jacob understood exactly what his father meant by that. So can you if you remember driving through the country when hay or wheat has been harvested recently. Particularly with the morning dew on the ground, or after a rain shower, the smell of a newly cut field is as fresh and refreshing as a mountain spring.

Isaac also pictured his son as someone whom other people, including his own family, should greatly respect. "Let peoples serve you," he said, "and nations bow down to you" (v. 29).

In the United States today, no premium is placed on physically bowing before dignitaries. About the only people who know how to bow anymore are actors and orchestra conductors. Most of us would have to practice for hours to bow properly if we were going to meet a visiting king or queen. In Isaac's day, however, bowing was a mark of respect and honor, something that was expected in the presence of an important person.

We can't miss the idea in these two pictures of praise that Isaac thought his son was very valuable, someone who had great worth. This message is exactly what modern-day children need to hear from their parents.

The Key to Communicating Value

Telling children they are valuable can be difficult for many parents, especially if the parents never heard such words when they were young. Besides, as we saw in a previous chapter, the just-right time to say such important words can get crowded out by the urgent demands of a busy schedule.

Some children do hear the obligatory "I love you" during holidays or at the airport, but it seems stiff and out of place. Other children may hear an occasional word of praise, but only if they perform well on a task. When words of value are only linked to a child's efforts to obtain a blessing, the child retains a nagging uncertainty about whether they ever really received it. If their performance ever drops even a small amount, that child may ask and ask again, "Am I loved for who I am or only for what I can do?"

We need to find a better way to communicate a message of high value and acceptance, a way to express a person's valuable qualities and character traits apart from their performance. Hidden inside the family blessing is a key to communicating such feelings to our children, spouses, friends, or church families, a key that we can perfect with only a little practice and that even gets around the walls a defensive adult or child can set up. This key is found in the way word pictures are used throughout the Scriptures.

The Power of a Picture

Positive or negative, word pictures are a useful communication tool because they are vivid and easy for most people to understand. They have an emotional impact that ordinary words may lack. That's why word pictures are so effective in giving a blessing.

We can see this clearly in the blessing Jacob used with three of his sons. Each is a beautiful example of how this communication tool can be used to attach high value to a child.

Jacob picked a different word picture for each of his sons to bestow the Blessing on them. We read, "This is what their father said to them when he blessed them. He blessed them, every one with the blessing appropriate to him" (Genesis 49:28 NASB).

"Judah is a lion's cub . . . and as a lion, who dares stir him up?" (49:9 NASB). Judah was depicted as a lion's cub. In the Scriptures a lion portrayed strength, and the lion was also a symbol of royalty in the ancient Near East.[3] Judah's leadership qualities and strength of character were illustrated by this picture.

"Naphtali is a doe let loose; he utters beautiful words" (49:21 NASB). Jacob pictured Naphtali as a doe. The grace and beauty of this gentle animal were used to show the artistic qualities this son possessed. He was the one who spoke and wrote beautiful words.

"Joseph is a fruitful branch, a fruitful branch by a spring" (49:22 NASB). Joseph was described as a fruitful branch by a spring. This word picture illustrated how Joseph's unfailing trust in the Lord allowed him to provide a place of refuge for his family. Jacob's word picture carries a similar message to one used first of Jesus in Psalm 1:3: "He will be like a tree planted by streams of water, which yields its fruit in its season, and its leaf does not wither; and in whatever he does, he prospers" (NASB).

Each of Jacob's sons was an individual, and each of them received a blessing that depicted his value to his father in the form of a word picture he could remember always. It's an example we would do well to follow when we give the Blessing. But before we rush off to call our child or spouse a lion, doe, or fruitful branch, we need to learn a little more about word pictures.

To do so, let's turn to a book in the Old Testament that is filled with them. While this book pictures a marriage relationship, the same principles can be used in giving children—or anyone else—the Blessing. Let's look at how this couple communicated words of love, acceptance, and praise. In doing so, we will discover four keys to communicating high value.

Word Pictures: Four Keys to Communicating High Value

In the Song of Solomon, God's picture of an ideal courtship and marriage, a loving couple praises each other using word pictures more than eighty times in eight short chapters. That's a lot! But they had a lot they wanted to communicate about how highly they valued each other and their relationship.

Let's begin our examination of how they used these descriptive words with each other by looking in on their wedding night. Not often is someone's wedding night written up for posterity, but this one is worth remembering. It is a vivid record of a loving, godly relationship.[4]

Seven times (the biblical number of perfection) Solomon praised his bride, who was altogether beautiful to him. He began his praise of her by saying, "Behold, you are fair, my love! Behold, you are fair! You have dove's eyes behind your veil" (Song of Solomon 4:1).

Key 1: Use an Everyday Object

What Solomon did with this word picture (and what wise parents do in blessing their children) was use an everyday object to capture a character trait or physical attribute of his beloved. In this case, he pictured her eyes as those of a dove. The gentle, shy, and tender nature of these creatures would be familiar to his bride. By picturing this familiar animal, Solomon was able to communicate far more meaning than he could by using words. (Words themselves are often one-dimensional, but a word picture can be multidimensional.) An added feature is that each time she saw a dove thereafter, she would be reminded of how her husband viewed her and valued her.

Key 2: Match the Emotional Meaning of the Trait You Are Praising with the Object You've Picked

Over and over Solomon used everyday objects that captured the emotional meaning behind the trait he wanted to praise. These objects may not be familiar to us, but they were familiar to his bride. Take, for example, his praise for his beloved just a few verses later. He looked at his bride and said, "Your neck is like the tower of David, built for an armory, on which hang a thousand bucklers, all shields of mighty men" (4:4).

Was Solomon trying to end his marriage before it began? Certainly not. Let's look at just how meaningful this analogy would have been to an insecure, blushing bride on her wedding night.

High above the old city of Jerusalem stood the Tower of David. A farmer working outside the city walls could look up from his work and see this imposing structure. What would impress him— even more than the height of this tower—was what hung from it.

Hanging on the tower during times of peace were the war shields of David's "mighty men"—King David's greatest warriors and the leaders of his armies. The sun shining off their shields would be a reassuring sight for one outside the protection of the city walls. By the same token, if that farmer looked up and saw that the shields of the mighty men had been taken off the tower, he would know it was time to hightail it inside the city walls! Danger was in the land.

Solomon comparing his bride's neck to David's Tower now begins to make a little more sense. In Old Testament times a person's neck stood for their appearance *and* attitude. That is why the Lord would call a disobedient Israel a "stiff-necked people" (Exodus 33:5). For Solomon, the peace and security represented in David's Tower provided a powerful illustration to express his love for his bride. He was praising the way she carried herself—with serenity and security.[5]

Key 3: Use Word Pictures to Unravel Defenses

Solomon took advantage of a third aspect of word pictures: the ability to get around the defenses of people who, for one reason or another, have a hard time hearing. This quality is something that a parent, spouse, or friend can use today. Whether we are dealing with defensive people or those who battle insecurity, using a word picture can help us get around their resistance and communicate high value to them.

Let's look first at how a word picture can encourage an insecure person. We can see this with Solomon's bride herself, known in the Song of Solomon as the Shulamite woman.

Like most young women who would unexpectedly meet a dashing young king, the Shulamite woman was insecure about her appearance. When she first met Solomon, she said, "Do not look upon me, because I am dark, because the sun has tanned me" (Song of Solomon 1:6). But after she had been around Solomon for only a short time, she called herself "the rose of Sharon, and the lily of the valleys" (2:1). That is quite a change of perspective! How did it happen?

It happened because Solomon's word pictures made their way around his bride's defenses. If Solomon had simply said, "You're cute," her insecurity could have thrown up a dozen reasons why this matter-of-fact statement could not be true: "Maybe his eyesight is bad." "I bet he's been hunting for three months, and I'm the first woman he's seen." "Maybe my father paid him to say that." These same kinds of reasons are used by insecure people today to ward off any compliments they hear about themselves. But word pictures have the ability to capture people's attention in spite of their defenses.

How do we know word pictures really got through to Solomon's bride in their marriage? Just look at how her attitude changed over the course of their married life.

During their courtship, she viewed their relationship with a certain insecurity and possessiveness. These feelings are evident in the way she talked about their relationship: *"My beloved is mine, and I am his"* (2:16, italics added).

As their story continued after the wedding—and as she grew more secure in his love—watch the subtle but powerful change in how she viewed their relationship. Once they were married, she told the ladies of the court, *"I am my beloved's, and my beloved is mine"* (6:3, italics added). This statement shows a little more security.

Then, as their story draws to a close, she even said, *"I am my beloved's, and his desire is toward me"* (7:10, italics added). This final statement shows a lot more security than her view of their relationship just before their wedding night.

Why? The major reason is the way word pictures of praise and great value have brought security to an insecure woman's heart. Repeatedly (more than fifty times), Solomon expressed his high value for his bride by using word pictures, and his words gradually transformed her view of herself and their relationship.

Most people will listen to a message more intently when it comes packaged in a word picture. That is one reason Jesus used word pictures to communicate both praise and condemnation through his teachings and his parables. He would talk about being the Good Shepherd who watched over the flock, the Bread of Life that would provide spiritual nourishment. By speaking in word pictures, he was able to penetrate the walls of insecurity and mistrust these people had put up, because stories and images hold a key to our hearts that simple words do not.

Jesus' extended object lessons kept his audience's attention even when some, like the Pharisees, did not really hear what he was saying. That is another advantage of word pictures. They are not just effective in getting through to an insecure person. They can also be immensely helpful in getting around the defenses of someone who, for some reason, just does not want to listen.

Key 4: Use Word Pictures to Point Out a Person's Potential

A fourth reason for using word pictures is to illustrate the undeveloped traits of a person—qualities they may not acknowledge or even be aware of. Jesus did this in changing Simon's name to Peter, which literally means "rock" in Greek. Peter certainly didn't act like a rock of strength and stability when he tried to talk Jesus out of going to the cross, when he went to sleep in the garden, or when he denied Jesus three times. But Jesus knew Peter's heart and understood what he could become. After the resurrection, Peter did become the rock Jesus had pictured him to be.

A very well-known saying tells us that one picture is worth a thousand words. When we link a word picture with a message of high value, we multiply our message a thousand times. That is the amazing power of the third element of the Blessing.[2]

---

2. If this idea of word pictures is new to you or you need more examples and help with creating them, Gary Smalley and I wrote an entire book about word pictures. See Gary Smalley and John Trent, *The Language of Love* rev. ed. (Carol Stream, IL: Tyndale Publishers, 2018).

CHAPTER 7

The Fourth Element: Picturing a Special Future

When it comes to predictions about their future, children are literalists—particularly when they hear predictions from their parents, the most important people (from an earthly perspective) in their lives. This is why communicating a special future to a child is such an important part of giving the family blessing. But this element of the Blessing isn't just for children. Feeling and believing that the future is hopeful and something to look forward to can greatly affect anyone's attitude on life. By picturing a special future for our children, spouse, or friends, we are providing them with a clear light for their paths in life.

Have you ever been camping in the woods on a dark night? If you have, you probably remember what it's like to walk away from your campfire into the night. In only a few steps, darkness can seem to swallow you up. Turning around and walking back toward the fire is a great deal more reassuring than groping around in the dark. But if you light a lantern from that fire, you actually will be able to see your way on the dark path.

Words that picture a special future act like a campfire on a dark night. They can draw a person toward the warmth of genuine concern and fulfilled potential. They act like the lantern as well.

Instead of leaving us to stumble into a dark unknown, they can illuminate a pathway lined with hope and purpose.

Children (and others) begin to take steps down the positive pathway pictured for them when they hear words like these: "God has given you such a sensitive heart. I wouldn't be surprised if you end up helping a great many people as a coach or counselor when you get older" or "You are such a good helper. When you grow up and marry someday, you're going to be such a profound help to your wife (or husband) and family."

Of course, the opposite is true as well. If children hear only words that predict relationship problems or personal inadequacies, they can turn and travel down the hurtful path that has been pictured for them. This can happen if they hear statements like "You'd better hope you can find someone who can take care of you when you're older. You're so irresponsible you'll never be able to do anything for yourself" or "Why bother to study so much? You'll just get married and drop out of school anyway."

If you add up the incredible costs exacted from the children in some families, you can see how devastating picturing a negative future can be. You can also see why a blessing in the Scriptures puts such a high priority on picturing a special future for each child.

One more crucial thing as we begin to look closer at how to picture a special future for a loved one is to understand that in our world today, perhaps no element of the Blessing is more under attack than this one. Far too many children are growing up thinking—or being told—there is no future! No hope! There is no purpose in planning or preparing for life. In some cases it's climate fear. In other cases, it's fallout from the effects of the past worldwide pandemic.

As difficult at these challenges are, always keep in mind Jeremiah 29:11: "'For I know the plans I have for you,' declares the LORD, 'plans for prosperity and not for disaster, to give you a future and a hope'" (NASB).

That is as true today as it was when it was first written in the Old Testament.

Picturing a Special Future in Patriarchal Homes

In the Old Testament, picturing a special future for children was an important part of the formal family blessing. We can see this by looking at the words Isaac spoke to Jacob:

> Therefore may God give you
> Of the dew of heaven,
> Of the fatness of the earth,
> And plenty of grain and wine.
> Let peoples serve you,
> And nations bow down to you.
> Be master over your brethren,
> And let your mother's sons bow down to you.
> Cursed be everyone who curses you,
> And blessed be those who bless you!
> (Genesis 27:28–29)

When Isaac spoke these words, much of his son's blessing lay in the future. Jacob was not swamped with people wanting to bow down to him, and he had no land or flocks of his own that God could bless. Yet the picture gave him the security of knowing he had something to look forward to.

One generation later, Jacob's son Judah received a similar picture of a special future: "Judah, you are he whom your brothers shall praise; your hand shall be on the neck of your enemies; your father's children shall bow down before you" (Genesis 49:8). Like father, like son—Jacob passed down this part of the blessing. This blessing pictured a special future that would take years to become reality but offered Judah a special hope as each year unfolded.

As we mentioned in an earlier chapter, these patriarchs' words had a prophetic nature that is not a part of the Blessing today. We as parents cannot predict our children's futures with biblical accuracy, but we can provide them with the hope and direction that can lead to meaningful goals. As they begin to live up to these goals, they gain added security in an insecure world.

In Orthodox Jewish homes and services, the wish for a special future for each child is constantly present. At the synagogue, the rabbi often says to young boys, "May this little child grow to manhood. Even as he has entered into the Covenant, so may he enter into the study of Torah, into the wedding-canopy and into a life of good deeds."[1] In the home, family blessings are also interlaced with words that picture a special future.

I (John) saw this aspect of the Blessing clearly in a Jewish home I was invited to visit one Thanksgiving. By the time I arrived, almost forty people were preparing or waiting patiently for a scrumptious dinner. Three generations—grandparents, parents, and their children—had assembled for this special occasion.

When the meal was prepared and before it could be served, the patriarch of the family (the grandfather) gathered all the family together. He had all the men and their sons stand on one side of the living room and all the women and their daughters stand on the other side. He then went around the room, placing his hands on the head of every person and speaking to them. To each man, he said, "May God richly bless you, and may he make thee as Ephraim and Manasseh." And each woman received the words "May God richly bless you, and may you grow to be like Rebekah and Sarah."

From the oldest grown son to the youngest grandchild, this time of blessing pictured a special future for each person in the room—even me, a stranger to him. Far from being a meaningless ritual, it provided everyone with a warm wish for a fulfilling life in the years to come.

Bringing Out the Best in Those We Bless

Picturing a special future for a child, spouse, or friend can help bring out the best in their life. It gives that person a positive direction to strive toward and surrounds them with hope. We can see this very thing in our relationship with the Lord. Listen to the beautiful way the prophet Jeremiah assures us of the special future we have in our relationship with God: "For I know the thoughts that I think toward you, says the LORD, thoughts of peace and not of evil, to give you a future and a hope" (29:11).

Jesus also went to great lengths to assure his insecure disciples that they had a special future with him. During their last Passover meal together, Jesus made sure they knew their future together would not end at his death. "In My Father's house are many mansions," he told them, "if it were not so, I would have told you. I go to prepare a place for you. And if I go and prepare a place for you, I will come again and receive you to Myself; that where I am, there you may be also" (John 14:2–3).

Time and time again in the Bible, God gives us a picture of our special future with him. However, his written Word is not the only way God communicates this message to us. Scattered throughout nature are a number of physical pictures of spiritual truths, pictures that illustrate the importance of providing a special future for the ones we love.

Anyone who has ever watched a caterpillar emerge from its cocoon as a butterfly has seen such a picture. The caterpillar is probably not on anyone's list of the world's "ten most beautiful creatures." Yet a caterpillar has the potential to be transformed into a list-topping, beautiful butterfly. What does this have to do with the Blessing? Words that picture a special future for a child, spouse, or friend can act as agents of this kind of transformation in that individual's life.

Words really do have that kind of transforming power. The apostle Paul certainly thought so. The actual term for the transformation of a caterpillar to a butterfly is *metamorphosis*, based on a Greek word. Paul used this same Greek word in the book of Romans. He was aware that the world had tremendous power to squeeze and mold the saints in Rome into a godless image. To counter this, he told these young believers, "Be transformed by the renewing of your mind, that you may prove what is that good and acceptable and perfect will of God" (Romans 12:2).

What does it mean to be "transformed by the renewing of your mind"? One excellent New Testament commentator explains the concept this way: "Since men are transformed by the action of the mind, transformed by what they think, how important to have the organ of thought renewed!"[2] In other words, godly thoughts and thinking patterns have the ability to transform us into godly men or women rather than leaving us to be squeezed into the imperfect mold of the world. Let's see how this works with regard to the Blessing.

Children are filled with the potential to be all God intended them to be. It is as if the Lord places them on our doorstep one day, and we as parents are left as stewards of their abilities. During the years we have children in our homes, the words we speak to them can wrap around them like a cocoon. What we say can shape and develop them in a positive way.

Let's look at another important picture in nature that mirrors what happens when we bless our children with words of a special future. This picture, explained to me by my twin brother, Jeff, a doctor in the field of cancer research, is found in something that happens in every cell in our bodies.[3]

Imagine a typical cell in your body by thinking of a circle. Attached to the outside of this circle are a number of receptor points. You could picture these receptor points as little squares that almost look like gears on a wheel. To make things easier to understand, picture these receptor sites as little square people.

Floating around near the cell are hormones and enzymes.

Think of them as Harry Hormone and Ethyl Enzyme, who would each love to shake hands with (or activate) these little receptor people. And while a great number of these hormones and enzymes have the ability to connect with a receptor site, some have a special ability to stimulate a cell's activity and cause it to work harder.

You can picture this special ability as someone coming up to you and shaking your hand up and down so vigorously that your whole body shakes and you feel energized. In fact, your neighbors start shaking and feel energized too. Such stimulation by hormones and enzymes, which causes the receptor sites to work harder, is called *positive cooperativity*.

But other hormones and enzymes act in a negative way when they shake hands with a receptor site. This is *negative cooperativity*. Have you ever had your hand squeezed so hard that you almost crumpled over in pain? That's the kind of thing that happens when these hormones and enzymes grab hold of a receptor site. In fact, not only does this one receptor site shut down and stop working because its "hand" is being squeezed, but all the receptor sites around it stop too.

And this applies to the Blessing . . . how?

Words that picture a special future for a child act like positive hormones that attach themselves to a cell. They stimulate all kinds of positive feelings and decisions within a child that can help them grow and develop. Words of a special future can inspire a child to work on a particular talent, have the confidence to try out for a school office, or even share their faith with other children.

But just like the negative hormones that shut down cell activity, a critical, negative picture of the future can crush or pinch off healthy growth in a child. Emotional, physical, and even spiritual growth in a child can be stunted because of the stifling effect of a negative picture of the future.

The Power of Past Consistency

By now you know how important it is to provide our children with words that point out a special future for them. But words alone may not be enough to get this message across to those we want to bless. Unless our words of a special future are backed up by a consistent track record, the person we are trying to bless may be unwilling or unable to believe what we say.

If we are serious about offering a message of a special future to our children, we need to follow the example the Lord sets. His consistency in the past acts as a solid footing on which words of a special future can stand.

Throughout the Scriptures the basis for believing God's Word in the future lies in his consistency in fulfilling his Word in the past. In Psalm 105:5 we read, "Remember His marvelous works which He has done, His wonders, and the judgments of His mouth." And in Psalm 33:9 the psalmist wrote, "He spoke, and it was done; He commanded, and it stood fast."

Because God has been reliable in the past, his words of a special future for us in the present have credence. The same principle applies to our desire to picture a special future for those we wish to bless. Our credibility in the past—or lack of it—will directly affect how our words are received in the present.

Perhaps your past has been anything but consistent with those you want to bless. Today really *is* the first day of the rest of your life. And by honoring commitments to your children today, you can begin to build the kind of history that words of a special future need to rest on. Remember, there is no such thing as "quality time" that makes up for inconsistency in your relationships. You need to have a track record of daily decisions that demonstrate your commitment to your children, your spouse, or anyone you would bless. Only then will your words of a special future really find their mark.

The Power of Present Commitment

As we've mentioned, if our words of a special future are to take hold and grow, we need to demonstrate commitment in the present. This idea of commitment is so important that we will spend the next chapter examining it in depth. However, one aspect of a present commitment applies directly to picturing a special future. The effectiveness of our predictions depends on the degree of certainty our children have that we will be around long enough to see those predictions come to pass.

Are you providing your children, spouse, or intimate friends with a blessing that pictures a special future for them? Did your parents take the time and effort to provide you with the hope of a bright tomorrow as you grew up? Wherever the Blessing is given or received, words that picture a special future are always shared—words that represent the fourth element of the Blessing.

CHAPTER 8

The Fifth Element: An Active, Genuine Commitment

In the past several chapters we have looked at the first four elements of the Blessing:

1. Appropriate meaningful touch
2. A spoken (or written) message
3. Attaching high value
4. Picturing a special future

These four elements are the building blocks of the Blessing. But the mortar that holds them together is an active, genuine commitment—the fifth element of the Blessing.

Why is an active, genuine commitment such an important part of the Blessing? As we have seen in earlier chapters, words of blessing alone are not enough. They need to be backed by an ongoing dedication to see the Blessing come to pass.

This principle is what the apostle James wanted us to understand in his letter. There we read, "If a brother or sister is naked and destitute of daily food, and one of you says to them, 'Depart in peace, be warmed and filled,' but you do not give them the things which are needed for the body, what does it profit?" (James 2:15–16).

To answer the apostle's question, words without commitment are about as useful as a crooked politician's promises on the eve of Election Day. Giving the Blessing involves action, linked to our words. If we *talk the talk* but then fail to put the elements of the Blessing into practice, we leave our children, spouses, and friends undernourished and ill-clothed in their need for love and acceptance.

The Blessing as found in Scripture offers a strong contrast to speaking empty words to our loved ones. It features several important steps we can take to demonstrate an active, genuine commitment to those we want to bless.

Step 1: Ask the Lord to Confirm the Blessing

When you look at the Blessing in the Old Testament, something that stands out is the way the patriarchs committed their children to the Lord. When Isaac blessed Jacob, we read, "May *God* give you of the dew of heaven, of the fatness of the earth" (Genesis 27:28, italics added). Years later, when Jacob blessed his sons and grandchildren, he began by saying, "The *God* who has been my shepherd all my life to this day . . . bless the boys" (Genesis 48:15–16 NASB, italics added).

One reason these patriarchs called on God to confirm their child's blessing was they were sure of his commitment to them. We can see this clearly with Isaac and Jacob.

In Genesis 26, Isaac was facing real problems. Living in the desert, he knew that his most precious assets were the wells he dug for fresh water. Twice Isaac had been driven from wells his father had dug. He was then forced to dig a third well to provide water for his flocks and his family. That night, as if to assure Isaac of his future in this land, "the LORD appeared to him . . . and said, 'I am the *God* of your father Abraham; do not fear, for I am with you. I will bless you and multiply your descendants'" (Genesis 26:24 NASB, italics added).

Isaac had been driven away from two wells that rightfully belonged to him. Hearing his heavenly Father declare his ongoing commitment to Isaac's family must have been like drinking cool, refreshing water on a hot summer's day.

God also echoed those words of commitment to Jacob at a difficult time in his life. Fleeing his brother Esau's anger, Jacob stopped one night to sleep out in the desert. It was there that God spoke to him and said, "I am the LORD God of Abraham your father and the God of Isaac. . . . Behold, I am with you and will keep you wherever you go, and will bring you back to this land; for I will not leave you until I have done what I have spoken to you" (Genesis 28:13, 15).

Isaac and Jacob were sure of their relationships with God. A natural extension of that certainty was to ask the Lord to bless their children through them. This is something we frequently see in churches today.

This past Sunday, in churches all across the country, pastors closed their services with the words "May the Lord bless you and keep you." By linking God's name to the blessing they spoke, these pastors were asking God himself to be the one to confirm it with his power and might—the very thing Isaac and Jacob did with their children.

We see the same idea in the dedication of children at a church. Often the pastor will lay his hands on children and say similar words of blessing, picturing the desire the parents and the entire congregation have in asking God to bless these little ones.

Wise parents will follow this practice in bestowing the Blessing on their children. When they say, "May the Lord bless you," they are first recognizing and acknowledging that any strength they have to bestow the Blessing comes from an all-powerful God. Even the very breath of life they have to speak words of blessing comes from him.

None of us are perfect parents. We are all prone to be inconsistent, and we stumble occasionally in providing the elements of the Blessing for our children. In contrast, God remains changeless in his ability to give us the strength to love our spouses and children the way we should.

A second important reason to commit our children to the Lord when we bless them is that doing so teaches them that God is personally concerned with their lives and welfare. Stressing that the Lord is interested in their being blessed is like introducing them to someone who can be their best friend, a personal encourager they can draw close to throughout their lives.

Children need the certainty and security that comes from committing them and their blessing to the Lord. That does not mean that we do not participate in the Blessing. Rather, it means that we recognize and acknowledge that only by God's strength and might will we ever be able to sustain our commitment to truly bless our children.

Step 2: Seek the Best Interest of the One Being Blessed

How do we begin committing ourselves to our children's best interests? First, as we have noted throughout the book, we must dedicate our time, energy, and resources to caring for them and spending time with them. However, Jacob observed another important principle in blessing his children. He recognized that every one of his children was unique.

In Genesis 48 and 49, Jacob (now called Israel) pronounced a blessing for each of his twelve sons and two of his grandchildren. After he finished blessing each child, we read, "This is what their father [Jacob] said to them when he blessed them. He blessed them, *every one* with the blessing appropriate to him" (Genesis 49:28 NASB, italics added).

Most of us are familiar with the verse "Train up a child in the way he should go, and when he is old he will not depart from it" (Proverbs 22:6). However, another helpful way to view this verse would be to translate it as "Train up a child according to his bent . . ."[1] In training (or blessing) a child, we need to take a personal interest in each child. The better we know our children and their unique set of needs, the better we will be able to give them their own unique blessing.

Please pay close attention to this next statement: physical proximity does not equal personal knowledge. We can spend years under the same roof with our spouses and children and still be intimate strangers. Many people feel as though they know another person's interests and opinions because they took an active interest in their lives in the past. However, people's thoughts, dreams, and desires can change over the years. Doctors tell us that every cell in our body wears out and is replaced by new cells within a few years. We are constantly changing both physically and emotionally.

In our homes we can be close in terms of proximity to one

another but far away in terms of understanding another person's real desires, needs, goals, hopes, and fears. However, we can combat this distance by taking the time to observe and understand the unique aspects of those we wish to bless.

Blessing our children involves understanding their unique bents. In addition, it means being willing to do what is best for those children, even if it means having to correct them when they are wrong.

Step 3: Discipline When Appropriate

Discipline may seem the very opposite of blessing another person. But in actuality, we bless our children by providing them with appropriate discipline. We see this when we look back at the individual blessings Jacob gave to each of his children.

Genesis 49 records a blessing for each son. However, at first glance the blessing that Reuben, the oldest son, received looks more like a curse than a blessing. Yet Jacob dealt with each son individually, and in Reuben's case his blessing included discipline as well as praise:

> Reuben, you are my firstborn,
> My might and the beginning of my strength,
> Preeminent in dignity and preeminent in
>   power.
> Uncontrollable as water, you shall not have
>   preeminence,
> Because you went up to your father's bed;
> Then you defiled it. (Genesis 49:3–4 NASB)

If we look closely at these verses, Jacob balances words of praise with words of correction. Reuben had several positive qualities his father praised (his might, strength, dignity, and power). However, he also had a glaring lack of discipline in his life. His unbridled passions led him to the bed of one of his father's concubines. As a result he was disciplined for his actions.

It should not surprise us that blessing and discipline go hand in hand. If we genuinely love someone, we will not allow that person to stray into sin or be hurt in some way without trying to correct them. This lesson was explained by the writer of Hebrews when he said, "MY SON, DO NOT REGARD LIGHTLY THE DISCIPLINE OF THE LORD . . . FOR WHOM THE LORD LOVES HE DISCIPLINES" (12:5–6 NASB).

God actively deals with our wrong behavior rather than merely ignoring it because he sees us as his beloved children. Parents are naturally more concerned about the behavior of their own offspring than they are about other people's children. Like a loving parent with a highly valued child, God does care about our behavior.

Our children's actions should also concern us if we are going to be a person who truly blesses them. We should not shy away from including loving discipline when it is appropriate and in their best interests.[2]

Initially, discipline can seem painful for both parents and children. Yet taking that risk can help bring out the best in children's lives by training them and guiding them to a place of peace and righteousness (Hebrews 12:11). Discipline is an important way of actively committing ourselves to a child's best interest.

We have looked at three ways in which we can demonstrate an active, genuine commitment in blessing others: we can commit them to the Lord, we can seek their best interests, and we can apply appropriate discipline. A fourth way to show an active, genuine commitment is something I have seen modeled all my life.

Step 4: Become a Student of Those You Wish to Bless

One thing that can greatly help us learn to become students of our children is to be lovingly persistent in communicating with them. Particularly if we have struggled in our relationships with our children or we haven't been close to them in the past, getting them to open up with us can take loving persistence. That doesn't mean badgering them or trying to pry the words out of their mouths. But it does mean consistently setting up times with them when meaningful communication can develop.

Second, realize that any shared activity with your children—from driving them to school or athletic practice to an airplane trip before they put on their headphones—offers tremendous opportunities to learn about them.

And taking the initiative in asking questions can be a third important way to become students of your children. Don't grill your child with questions as if you were giving a test. Just ask some casual questions in an offhand way, and then really listen to the answers.

Ask Your Children

Possible questions you can ask in those unguarded times at the hamburger place, at the ball game, or while taking a walk:

1. What do you daydream about most often?
2. What would you really enjoy doing when you are a young adult (twenty to thirty)?
3. Of all the people you have studied in the Bible, who would you most want to be like? Why?
4. What do you believe God wants you to do for humankind?
5. What type of boyfriend or girlfriend are you most attracted to, and why?
6. What is the best part of your school day? What is the worst?

Listen with full attention—that is the fourth practical way to get started in becoming a student of those you wish to bless. You actually bless your children by being emotionally present when they talk to you rather than being preoccupied with something else.

Have you ever carried on an entire conversation with a child while absorbed in a television show or reading Facebook posts? "Uh-huh" or "That sounds good, honey" uttered with our eyes glued to a screen does not communicate acceptance to your children, nor does it help you become a student of what they want to share.

I once read an interesting research study. A number of college men were given ten pictures of college-aged women who were more or less equally attractive. Each student was then asked to rate the pictures from "most attractive" to "least attractive."

What these young men did not know was that five of the women had been given an eye-drop solution just before their pictures were taken. This solution dilated the pupils in their eyes—the same thing that happens naturally when we are really glad to see someone. The results of the study were just as we might expect. The girls with the "bright eyes" were chosen hands down as the five most attractive women.

Do our eyes light up when we listen to those we wish to bless? Our children or spouses will notice if they do or don't. If we're serious about communicating genuine commitment, we need to get serious about putting down the smartphone or pausing (or turning off) the television when we talk to our loved ones and taking an active interest in their pursuits. Active listening is an important part of communicating acceptance and blessing, particularly genuine commitment.

Those of us who are parents need to realize that our children are incredibly complicated people. So are our wives or husbands and our friends. If we would begin today to list all their wishes, opinions, goals, and dreams, it would take us a lifetime to complete the task. That is just the right amount of time needed to finish the course titled "Becoming a Student of Your Loved Ones," a class men and women will enroll in if they are serious about bestowing an appropriate blessing to each person in their lives. All it takes to register is a decision to actively commit ourselves to others—and a pair of "bright eyes."

One Final Look at the Cost of Commitment

No doubt about it, commitment is costly. If you are serious about committing yourself to blessing those you love, expect to pay a price. Not necessarily in terms of money—a spouse and even small children are far too wise to be bought off with presents for very long. But you will need to invest time, energy, and effort to see the Blessing become a reality in their lives.

Is the price worth it? The book of Proverbs certainly seems to show us that it is. The final chapter of Proverbs describes a woman who blesses her family in many ways. She is industrious and loving, has a positive outlook on the future, and is committed to her husband and children. Her words to her family are filled with wisdom and kindness.

Did she just happen to be born this way? Certainly not. Each of these qualities was developed at a price. What is often skipped over when this passage is taught is how often this woman was up at dawn and how hard she worked to bless her family with her actions and words. She used the same kind of energy that gets parents out of bed on the weekend to take their children camping or enables a husband or wife to stay up late to help their spouse complete a project.

Was blessing her family really worth all that effort? It was for this woman. Read what her family has to say about her and her decision to make a genuine commitment to them: "Her children rise up and call her blessed; her husband also, and he praises her: 'Many daughters have done well, but you excel them all'" (Proverbs 31:28–29).

It takes hard work, wrapped in the words *active, genuine commitment*, to provide the Blessing to another person. It takes time to touch and hug our children meaningfully when they come home from school or before they go to bed. It takes courage to put into a spoken or written message those words of love for our spouses that have been on the tips of our tongues. It takes wisdom and boldness to "bow our knees" and highly value those we love. It takes creativity to picture a future for them filled with hope and with God's best for their lives. But all this effort is worthwhile.

One day, perhaps years later, the blessing that you give will return. Those you bless will rise up and bless you. What's more, you will find that the joy of seeing another person's life bloom and grow because of your commitment to seek their best is a blessing in itself.

CHAPTER 9

Your Blessing Day Begins with a Written Blessing

It's time. Not just to learn about the Blessing but also to take steps to give it. This is where Kari and I at StrongFamilies have joined with Joe Pellegrino at Legacy Minded Men to launch a worldwide challenge. It's called The Blessing Day.[1] This day can be any day you choose to make the choice to Bless.

It begins with this book to learn about the Blessing. It's not just for information. It's also about sharing your Blessing. You might ask, How do you build a Blessing?

In the next section of this book, we'll get specific on giving the Blessing to a particular person (a child, spouse, parent, or friend). But as we have seen in earlier chapters, it's the words you share that are important in giving the Blessing. For several reasons, we suggest that you put your words of blessing into written form first before you share them out loud with your child or capture them on video.

Why go so old school by writing out your Blessing?

---

1. When you finish this book, we'd love for you to take up the challenge of The Blessing Day and set aside a day to bless your family. Don't just stop with your home, but invite your small group, church, or team to learn about the Blessing. Consider writing or recording a Blessing for someone who really needs it. Go to StrongFamilies.com or TheBlessingDay.org for more information on how to help this generation deeply in need of the Blessing.

First of all, ideally, your written blessing will also be spoken to that child as you sit next to them in person. Or if they're far away, you'll capture it on video. Putting your Blessing in writing first can release a lot of pressure. It gives you the opportunity to put the words together at your leisure. You can double-check that you have included all the elements of the Blessing and that your words convey exactly what you want. And if your words have been chosen ahead of time when you do speak your blessing, you can concentrate on connecting with your child, giving them those "bright eyes."

Another reason to write out your blessing, though, is that a written blessing can be saved. It's your handwriting. And no matter how terrible or elegant it is, it's something from you and unique. Also, written words can be read and reread, and the paper it is written on can be tucked away as a keepsake. Yes, a typed and emailed blessing can be stored and reread. But handwritten blessings can be sent by letter or attached to an email and thus cover great distances. A written blessing has the capacity to bring warmth and light and love to your child again and again throughout their lives—far beyond the mere ink marks on paper.

Keep in mind that there is no wrong way to craft a blessing, and there are lots of creative right ways. And whether it comes out all at once in a rush of words or takes you a few tries and several evenings to outline and polish what you want to say, your child will cherish both what you write and what it represents about your relationship.

How you actually do the writing depends on what you are comfortable with. Some people work best in pencil on a yellow legal pad. Others can't even think without their iPad or laptop. You could even talk into a voice recorder and then transcribe your words.

And what should you say? Your words can be plain or poetic. They just need to carry with them a picture of your blessing that can help your child know that they are of high value to you. Here are a couple of examples to inspire you:

A Poetic Blessing

If you lean toward the creative or romantic side, then perhaps you can draw inspiration from this letter of blessing below. It was written by a father to his young daughter and given to her on June 11, 1948, when she was twelve years old. Today, more than fifty years later, it is still very much worth reading. I'll share the letter first; then I'll tell you who wrote it:

Dearest Joanne,

Those beautiful quaking aspens that you've seen in the forest as we have driven along have one purpose in life. I would like to tell you about them because they remind me a lot of Mommy and you kids and me.

Those aspens are born and grown just to protect the spruce tree when it's born. As the spruce tree grows bigger and bigger the aspens gradually grow old and tired and they even die after a while. But the spruce, which has had its tender self protected in its childhood, grows into one of the forest's most wonderful trees.

Now think about Mommy and me as aspens standing there quaking ourselves in the winds that blow, catching the cold snows of life, bearing the hot rays of the sun, all to protect you from those things until you are strong enough and wise enough to do it yourself. We aren't quaking from fear, but from the joy of being able to see your life develop and grow into tall straight men and women.

Just like the spruce, you have almost reached the point where you don't need us as much as you used to. Now you stand, like the young spruce, a pretty, straight young thing whose head is beginning to peep above the protection of Mommy and Daddy's watchfulness. . . .

I am telling you all this because from now on a lot of what you eventually become—a lovely woman, a happy woman and a brilliant, popular woman—depends on you.

You can't go through life being these things and at the same time frowning. You can't achieve these things and be grumpy. You have to grow so that your every deed and look reflect the glory that is now in your heart and soul.

Smile. Think right. Believe in God and His worldwide forest of men and women.

It's up to you.

> I love you,
> Daddy[1]

That's quite a letter, isn't it? In fact, in reflecting on it, his daughter Joanne states, "I still cry every time I read it. He was a master with words. He was a romantic."[2]

And who was Joanne's father? He wasn't a poet, pastor, or

teacher. He was a *politician*—Barry Goldwater. In fact, he is usually named as among the most hard-nosed of politicians. When he ran for president in the 1960s, he was demonized and said to be heartless. But that is not the side his daughter saw.

My point here isn't political. It is deeply personal. It's about the words that Goldwater wrote to his young daughter at a turning point in her life. I'm not saying Goldwater knew about the five elements of the Blessing as he wrote them—but reread it and just look at how many elements are there.

He pictures for her a positive future. He praises his daughter in words that demonstrate a genuine commitment. He attaches high value to her even during a difficult period in her life. (For most of us, keeping a good attitude during adolescence is tough.) With the exception of appropriate meaningful touch—which is hard to provide in a letter if he didn't hand it to her or sit next to her while she read it—that letter includes every element of the biblical blessing. No wonder it still means so much to her.

So feel free, in writing your blessing for your child, to be poetic like that hard-nosed politician. But don't worry if you are more the practical, straightforward sort. You don't have to be a poet to give a meaningful blessing—as another letter shows us.

Practical Words of Praise

"Dear Michael," writes an engineer who thought long and hard before writing out a much more practical but just as precious letter to his newborn son:

As I sit beside you, and read you this letter today, I hope you'll know how much time and thought I've put into each word. After all, it's been nine long months, one week, and two days since we found out you were coming! I want you to know, today and always, that we prayed for you before you were born. That every day you were in Mommy's tummy, we prayed for you. And I want you to know that on this day when they handed you to me, the day of your birth, I had tears in my eyes and had to sit down, I was so filled with joy. We are so grateful to God for you, and so committed to being the best parents we can for you and God. This letter is the first official "birthday blessing" letter that I'm committed to writing you. Each year, as God gives me strength and life, I'll write more about why I love you, why you're so special to me, and why I'm so glad and honored to be your dad.

Your Dad[3]

You would think there wouldn't be very many words to bless a child only a few hours old, but that letter says so much so well. And so will your letter to your child. Whether your child is twelve years or twelve hours old, whether your blessing is handwritten or typed out, whether you can write elegant prose or can barely spell—none of that matters. It's the words that count, and the time is now!

Sharing Your Blessing with Your Child

Once you have written your words of blessing, they can be a power-ful "memorial marker" for your child. We encourage you to talk with your spouse (if you're married) and pick a special time and place to share these words with your child. If at all possible, do it face-to-face. Pick a meaningful time, place, or event—a family affair with lots of friends and relatives, a milestone celebration such as a birth or graduation, or a quiet dinner with just the two of you. Just make sure that it is at a time and place that allows you to be quiet long enough to read or recite the blessing you have written to your son or daughter.

Don't forget to include the element of meaningful, appropri-ate touch along with your blessing—a hand on the head, an arm around the shoulder, and hopefully a big hug. You might even want to snap a picture of the two of you together or give the child a keep-sake copy of your blessing done in a special font, calligraphy, or just your best handwriting.

What if you can't be physically present—if you are deployed overseas, for instance, or divorced and living across the country? If you will be together soon, why not write out your blessing now and wait until you are together to deliver it? But don't wait too long. You can always write out your blessing in your best handwriting or format it on the computer and put it in the mail. We encourage you to write it out first, capture a video of your blessing, and then email it to your child or do the whole thing live via video services.

Keep in mind that there is no wrong way of giving a child

your blessing. Even if you choose to do a special dinner and burn the hamburgers, if it rains on the one night you have counted on a starlit sky, if the dog decides to throw up just before the special event, or if the camera batteries fail, it doesn't really matter. If you will write down your words and make your plans, we believe you will find that God just works it out!

The fact that your child receives your blessing is far more important than any challenges you face in delivering it. It is your blessing, prepared just for them. And however you choose to deliver it, make sure your child has a copy of your written words or a video you captured for their Blessing Day. A letter that perhaps they will keep and carry along to college or out into the world. If it's a video, they will keep looking at your blessing during those tough days head.

A Lifetime of Blessing

Don't wait! Don't leave your blessing to chance! Make an intentional plan to give your son, your daughter—everyone you care about—your blessing. Write it down. Speak the words. Make a video. Make a memory now and give it as a keepsake for tomorrow.

But don't stop there.

The kind of planned, formal blessing we have described in this chapter can be wonderful and life-changing, but if you really want your child to thrive, you will not only *give* the Blessing but also *live* it, seeking out ways to include appropriate meaningful touch, spoken and written words, messages of high value and a special future, and evidence of active, genuine commitment in every day you spend together.

At the breakfast table and over bedtime prayers, some parents memorize a little blessing to say or sing to their children. In the car on the way to school can be the perfect time for an offhand conversation with a teen. While on the soccer field, in the movie theater, at church, at the park, or in the backyard, look for ways to inject little words of blessing into everyday conversation.

Blessing Activity

Choose a time that will be your Blessing Day for that child you love. Write out or record a video of your Blessing for them.

PART 3

IMPLEMENTING THE BLESSING

CHAPTER 10

Your Blessing

Okay, now for the fun part! In order to truly live out the Blessing, there is one blessing that needs to happen first: yours.

To be fully free to bless, we first need to know—and believe—we are blessed ourselves.

If you've made it this far into the book, you have a good idea of whether you've received the Blessing. Sadly, many of us have not. Even if you did receive the Blessing, you may have realized that you are still struggling with either believing it or living it out. Still others of us are feeling thankful that we received the Blessing and can't wait to share it with others.

No matter where you are, before we ask you to bless others, we want to take a few minutes to make sure that *you* know you have the Blessing.

You might ask, Isn't that self-serving at best or, worse, just piling up personal accolades to build up pride? Actually, knowing you are blessed is the starting point for living out what's called "the Golden Rule" that Jesus talked about: "Do to others what you would have them do to you" (Matthew 7:12 NIV).

If you are working through this book on your own, we'd strongly encourage you to get someone to do this with you. Ask your spouse, best friend, pastor, coworker, or someone else you are close to. There is power in having someone you love speak life over you.

If you aren't ready to do that, or if there isn't someone you feel comfortable asking, that's okay. My dad and I (Kari) will be the ones speaking life over you today.

The purpose of this chapter is not just for you to hear the Blessing from someone else; it's for you to begin to speak words of life and blessing over yourself as well.

Before we jump into your blessing, there are a few things to keep in mind as you read and work through this chapter with your chosen friend or on your own:

1. It can be uncomfortable to receive this type of affirmation and blessing, especially if you have never experienced it before. It's okay to feel any emotion that comes up as you read this. We've heard it all—from no emotion at all to anger and disbelief, from tears and pain to laughter and joy. Feel whatever it is you need to feel. But no matter what that emotion is, keep rereading your blessing—out loud—until you "get it" in your heart.

2. If you are struggling with accepting this truth about yourself, one suggestion is to look in the mirror. Literally. Eight years ago, when I was at my lowest point, I didn't believe a single good thing about me existed. A dear friend of mine had me stand in front of the mirror and repeat truth about who I was and how much God loved me. At the time, I wanted to kick, scream, storm out of the room, and never talk to her again. However, I did it. And it changed my life.

To this day, I have truth in the form of verses hanging on my mirror and around my house to remind me to continue to speak blessings over myself.

It's amazing how hard it can be to bless ourselves. We often feel so free, and much more comfortable, doing this for others. But let me tell you: if you don't take the time to make sure that *you* know you are blessed and live from that place yourself, any blessing you share with others will always be a fraction of what it could be.

So here's how this chapter works: pick one or all of the blessings below and follow the process we have laid out for you. We have three categories of blessing for you to choose from:

1. I've never received the Blessing.
2. I need the Blessing for this season.
3. I got the Blessing, and I'm ready to bless.

Again, feel free to just read the option that applies to you or even all three!

I've Never Received the Blessing

If you are reading this and you have never received the Blessing, we are going to give you one right now.

If you are doing this with your spouse, friend, or coworker, get that person to read this out loud. If you are doing this on your own, you guessed it—read it out loud. Know that we (John and Kari) have prayed this over each person who is to pick up and read this book.

If you are the person reading this blessing for someone else, place your hand on the shoulder of the person who is to receive it. Read these words, all of which come right out of God's Word and are truths that *he* says about *you*:

- You are chosen.[1]
- You are wanted.[2]
- You are loved.[3]
- You are redeemed.[4]
- He has called you by name—and *you are his*.[5] Part of his family. His son. His daughter. His beloved.[6]
- There is nothing you have done, or ever can do, that will cause him to walk away from you.[7] He will never leave you.[8]
- He has created you with a *great* purpose on purpose.[9] And he has *great* plans for you: plans for your good—not your destruction. Plans for hope and a special future.[10]
- Every place that is broken, he will redeem and restore.[11] Every place that is rough, he will make smooth.[12] Every place there is doubt, fear, or confusion—be replaced with courage, peace, and wisdom in the name of Jesus.
- You are not alone. *We* choose you. The Lord chooses you. *You have our blessing.*
- You are blessed. You've been designed to bless. And right now, you are choosing to use your unique, God-given strengths to bless others as well.

Don't Skip This Step

Now, if you are the one receiving this blessing, it's your turn! Take a moment to read the same blessing out loud, replacing the word *you* with *I*. Reading the blessing out loud and declaring it for yourself are two key parts to moving knowledge from your head to your heart. If you are doing this with a friend, have them continue to stand with you and keep their hand on your shoulder in agreement. Read the following truth about who God Almighty says *you* are:

- I am chosen.
- I am wanted.
- I am loved.
- I am redeemed.
- He has called me by name—and *I am his*. Part of his family. His son. His daughter. His beloved.
- There is nothing I have done, or ever can do, that will cause him to walk away from me. He will never leave me.
- He has created me with a *great* purpose on purpose. He has *great* plans for me: plans for my good—not for my destruction. Plans for hope and a special future.
- Every place that is broken, he will redeem and restore. Every place that is rough, he will make smooth. Every place there is doubt, fear, or confusion—be replaced with courage, peace, and wisdom in the name of Jesus.
- I am not alone. I am chosen by the Lord, and by _____

_____

_____ (fill in as many names as you can think of here).

- I am blessed. I've been designed to bless. And I choose to use my unique, God-given strengths to bless _____ _____ (fill in names here) as well.

I Need a Blessing for This Season

Even if you've received the Blessing, there are many reasons why you may feel like you need some extra encouragement or a good reminder. Maybe you haven't heard the words in a long time. Or it's been a tough season, one where your circumstances or personal decisions have left you feeling discouraged or full of shame. No matter the reason, we all face times when we just need to hear the Blessing.

If you are doing this with your spouse or friend, get that person to read this out loud. If you are doing this on your own, you guessed it—read it out loud. Again, know that we (John and Kari) along with the Lord have prayed this over each person who is to pick up and read this book.

If you are the person reading this blessing, place your hand on the shoulder of the person who is to receive it. Read these words, all of which come right out of God's Word and are truths that *he* says about *you*:

- You are the Lord's.[13]
- He is proud of you.[14]
- He has designed you specifically as you are[15]—and has *great* plans for you.[16]
- He has created you to be a voice for his love.[17]

- You are able, through him, to love others like Jesus.[18]
- Nothing you've done, or ever will do, can remove his love from you.[19]
- Every place that's dry, be filled with living water.[20] Every place that's weary, be filled with strength.[21] Every hurt or disappointment, be turned to joy.[22] Every place of shame be covered in grace and be fully whole in the name of Jesus.
- You are blessed. You are loved. You are chosen. We choose you.
- And you can choose to bless others as well.

Don't Skip This Step

If you are the one receiving this blessing, it's your turn. Take a moment to read the blessing you just received out loud, replacing the word *you* with *I*. As you read it, ask the Lord to give you fresh encouragement and reminders about how much he loves you. Remember, there is power in our words, and saying them ourselves is part of making them our own. Those who are there to support you can keep their hands on your shoulders in agreement as you read as well:

- I am the Lord's.
- He is proud of me.
- He has designed me specifically as I am—and has *great* plans for me.
- He has created me to be a voice for his love.
- I am able, through him, to love others like Jesus.
- Nothing I've done, or ever will do, can remove his love from me.
- Every place that's dry, be filled with living water. Every

THE POWER OF THE BLESSING

place that's weary, be filled with strength. Every hurt or disappointment, be turned to joy. Every place of shame be covered in grace and be fully whole in the name of Jesus.

- I am blessed. I am loved. I am chosen by the Lord, and by

  _____

  _____ (fill in as many names as you can think of here).
- And I choose to bless _____ (fill in names here).

I Got the Blessing, and I'm Ready to Bless

If you got the Blessing and you're feeling great about jumping into blessing others, we still have a blessing for you. This blessing comes right out of Psalm 103.

If you are doing this with your spouse or friend, get that person to read this out loud. If you are doing this on your own, you guessed it—read it out loud. We (John and Kari) along with the Lord have prayed this over each person who is to pick up and read this book—and we know God wants to bless you.

If you are the person reading this blessing, place your hand on the shoulder of the person who is to receive it. Read these words, all of which come right out of God's Word and are truths that *he* says about *you*:

- Praise the LORD, my soul; all my inmost being, praise his holy name.
- Praise the LORD, my soul, and forget not all his benefits— who forgives all your sins and heals all your diseases, who

redeems your life from the pit and crowns you with love and compassion, who satisfies your desires with good things so that your youth is renewed like the eagle's.

- The LORD works righteousness and justice for all the oppressed.
- He made known his ways to Moses, his deeds to the people of Israel: The LORD is compassionate and gracious, slow to anger, abounding in love.
- He will not always accuse, nor will he harbor his anger forever; he does not treat us as our sins deserve or repay us according to our iniquities.
- For as high as the heavens are above the earth, so great is his love for those who fear him; as far as the east is from the west, so far has he removed our transgressions from us.
- As a father has compassion on his children, so the LORD has compassion on those who fear him. (Psalm 103:1–13 NIV)

Don't Skip This Step

If this is your blessing, it's time for you to read it out loud. Take a few moments to praise the Lord for all that he has done and continues to do for you:

- Praise the LORD, my soul; all my inmost being, praise his holy name.
- Praise the LORD, my soul, and forget not all his benefits— who forgives all [my] sins and heals all [my] diseases, who redeems [my] life from the pit and crowns [me] with love and compassion, who satisfies [my] desires with good things so that [my] youth is renewed like the eagle's.

- The LORD works righteousness and justice for all the oppressed.
- He made known his ways to Moses, his deeds to the people of Israel: the LORD is compassionate and gracious, slow to anger, abounding in love.
- He will not always accuse, nor will he harbor his anger forever; he does not treat [me] as [my] sins deserve or repay [me] according to [my] iniquities.
- For as high as the heavens are above the earth, so great is his love for [me] who fear[s] him; as far as the east is from the west, so far has he removed [my] transgressions from [me].
- As a father has compassion on his children, so the LORD has compassion on [me] who fear[s] him. (Psalm 103:1–13)

What's Next?

For some of you, that blessing was the first time you've been told the *truth* about who you are, your value, and the fact that someone—including Jesus—is crazy about you.

If you need to keep rereading any of the blessings above, do it! You can even order a print of any of these blessings at TheBlessing. com/store. Or feel free to rewrite it yourself. Hang it on your mirror. Put it in your car. Place it on your desk. Anytime the Enemy begins to tell you lies about who you are, who you're created to be, or if you really have value, read your blessing out loud.

Whether that was your first blessing or your hundredth, if you feel like you need more breakthrough in believing that you are chosen for a great purpose, dig in and get more help.

Here are a few ways we recommend you do that:

1. Find a great counselor. Or connect with us and find a Blessing Coach. My dad and I both, as well as our trained Blessing Coaches, offer coaching. And we are ready to help you. Visit StrongFamilies.com.
2. Take one of our Blessing courses. (We have several, including one on what to do if you didn't get the Blessing.)
3. Walk through this book with people you trust and process your feelings together.
4. Become one of our StrongFamilies "Blessing and Attachment" Coaches. Head to StrongFamilies.com and see how helping others receive and give the Blessing can be a tremendous blessing to you.

For many of us, it's a combination of these things that brings the breakthrough we need. The goal is to keep moving and, no matter what steps you choose, take a step toward blessing. It really does start with you.

Blessing Activity

Pick one of the blessings in the chapter.

Write down this blessing (or order the print from our website) and put it in a place where you will see it every day.

Every day, for the next thirty days, read it *out loud* to yourself.

CHAPTER 11

Blessing Your Kids and Grandkids

Many of you picked up this book because you want to know how to give your blessing to your kids or grandkids. This chapter will give you many practical ways to do just that.

Blessing Babies

Is it ever too early to start blessing? No! Just as babies can hear their parents' voices when they are still in the womb, these little ones can see, hear, and comprehend even more than we've previously given them credit for.

So what does it look like to bless your baby?

1. Use the Right Tone

Your baby may not be able to understand the meaning of your words, but research shows he absolutely understands your tone.[1] While the words may not be as important at this age, it is a *great* time to practice speaking blessings out loud and incorporating them into your daily routine.

110

2. Turn It into a Song

From YouTube videos to scientific journal articles, we've seen just how responsive babies are to music. Many babies even dance to or babble their own songs before they began speaking words.[2] By making up a blessing song and singing it again and again to your child, you are not only helping your little one learn but also giving her something she can participate in even before she says her first words.

3. Write It Down

They may not be able to read yet, but they will someday. The blessings you write down for your small children today not only will help you become more comfortable with sharing your blessing but also will be something your children get to read with you as they get older. In fact, I (Kari) have a book of blessings that I still keep on my nightstand. The blessings are all from my parents, starting from the day I was born all the way until today. These are letters I go back to again and again on hard days when I need encouragement or a reminder that I have their blessing.

When my son Lincoln was born, we had his grandparents, aunts, uncles, and other family members write him a blessing. They are framed and hanging on his wall next to a picture of the person who wrote it. Now that he's getting older, we read these blessings every night before bed. He gets so excited pointing out "Nanna, Bubba, Aunt Rara" and other key people in his life and hearing what they have to say about him, even if he doesn't understand all the words yet.

4. Use Your Smile

Babies as young as nine hours can already distinguish faces. At eleven hours, they can even tell the difference between their mom and a stranger. It's no surprise, then, that while it takes babies some time to identify voice tone with corresponding emotions (about five months is when this starts to occur), they prefer to look at smiling faces—even just hours after being born.[3] Studies also show that smiling builds trust, paints a picture of approval and security, and encourages your baby to explore the world around him. Plus, remember when we mentioned that "love moves at the speed of joy"? That's literally what your smile and bright eyes convey to your baby. That you are truly happy to see him.

So, to start your child off with a blessing and to help him feel confident and affirmed even hours after he is born—smile![4]

Blessing Young Kids

What does it look like to bless your younger children?

1. Tell Them a Story

I'll never forget being driven to school each morning—not because of the car ride but because of the stories my dad would tell. Each morning, from our first day of kindergarten through our last day of junior high, my dad would drive my best friend, Brynne, and me to school—and he would give us his blessing in the form of a story.

These stories often centered on our favorite character, Bungee

Bear, a super cute bear who had a bungee cord attached to him. Since Bungee Bear lived on a cloud, this bungee cord was especially helpful in ensuring that he would never fall out of his home. But it also kept him tied to something even more important—Jesus. Each day, Bungee Bear would face something that we were struggling with—from someone taking our lunch to friends being hurtful. And at the end of each story, as we were pulling into the drop-off zone, my dad would pray a blessing over us. He made sure that we knew—just like Bungee Bear—that our parents and the Lord were crazy about us and weren't going anywhere, no matter how challenging it got.

These Bungee Bear stories became such an important part of our lives that once a year, our dads, Brynne, and I would have a Bungee Bear breakfast. Brynne and I would get dressed up, grab one of our favorite stuffed bears, and go with our dads to a "fancy" restaurant (it was actually a cozy café located at the Scottsdale Airpark where we could watch the planes take off and land). Once we were there, our dads would tell us a Bungee Bear story and give us their blessing. Decades later, Brynne and I *still* remember Bungee Bear and our daily blessings. We've even asked our dads to continue to do grown-up Bungee Bear breakfasts with us (minus the teddy bears).

2. Pick Something They Love

No matter what your child loves, there's a way to relate it back to a blessing. Does your child love trains? Cars? Princesses? Bugs? Dinosaurs? Superheroes? Horses? Music? Sports? Art? Whatever it is that has captivated their affection, take a few minutes and follow the formula below to come up with a word picture that will help your child "get" your blessing.

> Hey [child's name], you really love [interest/thing], don't you? Well, you know how [interest/thing] makes you feel happy, excited, and is something you want around you all the time? That's exactly how I feel about you! In fact, I love you *even more* than you love [interest/thing]. And no matter what you love, or how grown-up you get, I'm always going to love you and be excited about how God has made you. And you know what else? Jesus is *even more* crazy about you than I am!

It's really that easy to help your child get the picture of how much you love them.

3. Plan at Date Night to Celebrate All Milestones

Brynne, my best friend I mentioned above, and her husband, John, took potty training their kids to the next level. When their beautiful daughter began the process of potty training, they told her that as soon as she had completed her potty-training chart, she would get to have a special date night with her dad. She sailed through her potty training, and on the day of her date with Daddy, they pulled out all the stops. They bought her a special dress, complete with "grown-up girl" shoes. Their daughter's favorite babysitter came over and did a special big-girl hairstyle. And John, being a true gentleman, showed up at the front door with a corsage for his daughter. He had also borrowed a special car for the evening, complete with a single flower waiting for her in her car seat.

John took their daughter to her favorite restaurant (where she could have pancakes for dinner), and while they were there, he gave her his blessing. When she got home, more surprises were waiting for her. Both sets of grandparents, several close friends, and Brynne were there in the decorated living room. They each gave her their blessing as well. While that may seem like a lot for a three-year-old, their daughter (now five) still talks about "date night with Daddy." And this is something they've replicated for other big achievements in her life as well.

4. Keep Singing

Just like babies, kids love music too! In fact, I can still sing you the blessing song my parents made up for me when I was young. Each morning when they woke me up for school, they would come into my room singing. The lyrics were:

> *Good morning, good morning, how are you today?*
> *The Lord bless you and keep you throughout the day.*
> *We love you, we love you, we love you, Kari.*

While that may sound super corny, when I was five, my parents saw firsthand how much that song meant to me. They were trying to put me to sleep one night, and I had crawled out of bed for the eighth time. After they had threatened everything except for monsters under the bed to try to get me to go to sleep, my little voice called down the hallway, "Good night, Mom! Good night, Dad! Don't forget to bless me in the morning!"

Even at five years old, I *wanted* my parents' blessing each morning. I longed for it. And your kids do too.

5. Use the Special Plate

When I was growing up, there was no greater sign of achievement or accomplishment in our house than getting to eat dinner with the Special Plate. The Special Plate has a long history in my family, and it can in yours as well.

The Special Plate first made an appearance the day I was born. Donna, a good friend of our family, showed up at the hospital not with baby clothes, flowers, or balloons but with a box containing a red china plate with the words *You Are Special Today* written across it. She told my parents to use this as a way to bless me as I was growing up. Four years later, when my sister, Laura, was born, Donna showed up with a second *You Are Special Today* plate.

As a kid, there was no higher honor in our home than getting to eat dinner on the Special Plate.

The reality was we got the Special Plate *a lot*. We got the Special Plate on our first day of school, for doing an extra chore to help at home, for completing a hard homework assignment, for defending a friend who wasn't being treated kindly, for trying our hardest even if we didn't make the team, for making a hard decision, and so on.

While to some it may seem that we overused the Special Plate, it never felt like that. Each time we were the recipient of that beautiful red plate, my mom and dad would tell us that we had their blessing and that they would always be there as we continued to become the women God had created us to be.

When Joey and I got married, I got a package in the mail from Donna. When I opened it, tears flooded my eyes. Inside was my very own red *You Are Special Today* plate. It's been a blessing to continue to use the Special Plate with Joey, and now our two sons, to celebrate key moments in our lives and the commitment to bless and help each other grow as well.

If you like the idea of a Special Plate for your family, you can get your very own Special Plate, exactly like the one we have, at this link: StrongFamilies.com/living-the-blessing/the-special-plate.

Blessing Older Kids

What does it look like to bless children who are older?

1. Leave a Message

I used to *love* parent-teacher "back to school" night at the beginning of the school year—not because I wanted my parents to meet my teacher but because I knew the next day was going to be a *great* day. This was because the night before, while my parents traveled to my different classrooms, they were also leaving a trail of notes for me.

Starting in kindergarten and going through my senior year of high school, my parents would hide encouraging notes for me in places where I would find them throughout the year.

Some were in my pencil box, and others waited in books, my cubby, art supplies, inside my locker, or even taped to my seat for me to find first thing in the morning.

My parents were so devoted to this practice that they actually got in trouble for passing notes during parent-teacher night one year.

I may not have been crazy about going to school the next morning, but I *was crazy* about finding my parents' notes. And the ones that were better hidden always seemed to make an appearance on days when I really needed them.

Notes like these don't need to be long or wordy. In fact, ours were always written on sticky notes. Even a "We are super proud of you—Love, Mom and Dad" or "You are going to change the world with your words" in an English book can add so much life to your child. Really, just a few notes of encouragement for your kids can go a long way.

2. Make Traveling Special

Growing up, my dad traveled a lot. But I can honestly tell you that while he was a million-miler with two different airlines, it *never* felt like it.

Whenever my dad went out of town, he took time before and after the trip to make sure we knew that he loved us.

Before he would leave, he would have Laura and I sit down at the kitchen table. He would pull out a placemat with a map of the United States on it. He would ask us where we lived, and we would point to Phoenix on the map. Then he would tell us what city he was flying to and help us find it on the map. He would then walk us through what he was going to do while he was there.

Now, let me pause here. You may think that kids don't really care about what their parents do for work. But you're wrong. To most kids, when their parents travel for work, it's like a black hole.

They don't know where their parents are, what they are doing, or if it's really even important. Taking a few minutes to walk your kids through your trip can change that.

For us, when my dad would show us where he was going and briefly describe what he would be doing—we got the picture. We realized the trips were intentional, he was doing something important, and we knew exactly where he would be. It added both peace and security for Laura and me and made us feel like our dad wanted us to be a part of what he was doing when he wasn't at home.

I'm not saying you need to go into great detail about your meetings or get into the technical aspects of your job. But a simple "I'm flying to Omaha, and I have meetings with some important people about our new project all day Tuesday, and I have a big lunch with my boss on Wednesday before I fly home" can be super helpful for your kids. You can even ask your kids to be praying for you and your meetings, projects, presentations, and more as you travel!

When my dad got home, Laura and I would race to the door, because we knew something special was coming . . . we would get a surprise! These surprises were small, inexpensive gifts that my dad would bring home from his trip. Think of a rock, postcard, or even sometimes a complimentary lotion from the hotel he had stayed at. While they were small gifts, and often disregarded after a few minutes, they let us know that he had been thinking about us while he was gone. However, there was a catch. Before we got our gifts, he would sit down with us and tell us about his trip. Again, this wasn't a long, detailed list of what he had done. It was an overview so that we knew, again, that he had been gone for a reason and that he had missed us while he was gone.

While that may sound like a lot, the real work came on the longer trips. Whenever my dad was gone for more than three days, or anytime he and my mom were traveling at the same time, Laura and I felt like it was Christmas.

Before they left, they would put out a brown lunch bag, one for each day they were gone, and number them 1, 2, 3, and so on for the total number of days they would be out of town.

Each morning before we got ready for school, Laura and I would race to our paper bag and open it with excitement. Inside would be a short note of encouragement, along with a small present.

Again, these weren't expensive gifts. Sometimes it was a pack of gum or a toy from the dollar store, or sometimes my dad would take a stuffed animal we already had and put it inside the bag with a short note about how he loved us more than we loved that animal.

The gifts weren't important. The important thing was, *each* day he or my mom was gone, we knew beyond a shadow of a doubt that they were thinking about us, missing us, and continuing to find ways to give us their blessing—even if they weren't able to be with us.

Okay, so now that you're totally overwhelmed, let's step back. Practically, this does take some planning, time, and effort. But if you travel a lot or even just a few times a year, let me tell you—there is no better way I've found to help your kids *know* you are with them, even when you can't physically be there.

I asked my dad how long planning this took, and he said he spent about five minutes the night before a short trip to tell us where he was going, plus an additional ten to fifteen minutes the night before a long trip to make the bags. In fact, my mom would buy small gifts at the dollar store and keep them in a hidden place in their closet so my dad could grab those when he needed them. So, next trip, as you pack, add in an extra ten minutes to bless your kids. You'll be glad you did.

3. Play Twenty Questions

Turn off the iPad or DVD player in the car and play Twenty Questions. While every family has their own rules for Twenty Questions, for us the game looked something like this:

- My parents would ask us a question. We would answer, and then we'd get to ask them a question.
- This would go on until we reached our destination—which usually involved some type of treat for us: a trip to the park, ice cream, or an hour to play before we had to start on our homework.

Playing Twenty Questions not only taught us how to communicate as a family but also taught us that we could ask our parents questions.

My parents would also end every session by reminding us that they would always want to know more about us—and that they were open to talking with us about any questions we might have.

Creating this type of safe environment for questions and communication early on will make it tremendously easier for your kids to relate to you as they enter the teen and adult years.

It's also a great tip to remember for older kids. We've all had this after-school conversation:

Us: Hey, honey, how was school today?
Them: Fine.
Us: Okay. What did you learn at school today?
Them: Nothing.
Us: Did you do anything fun?
Them: No.
Us: What did you do with your friends?
Them: Nothing.

Anyone else feeling the all-too-real pain of that conversation? The great thing about Twenty Questions is you get to be specific. Let them know that for their answer to count, it can't be one word—it needs to be a full sentence, and they need to ask you a question in return. You can also add in a bribe—think of a snack or activity that they enjoy—to get them to participate. That's right, in the Trent household we are not above bribing teenagers to talk to us . . . or do errands with us . . . or choose to continue to ride with us.

Blessing Teens

Here are some thoughts for blessing teenagers in your family.

1. Look at the Calendar

While this is something you can do with your kids at any age, or even with your spouse and friends, there is something about the teenage years that makes them heavily schedule driven. And once your teens start driving, it can seem like your entire family is hardly ever in the same place at the same time!

However, you can turn even the craziest schedule into a weekly blessing.

Here's what you do:

- Once a week, sit down as a family and talk about the upcoming week. At our house, this always seems to happen at Sunday dinner, since it's the one time we all end up at home—but you can pick any day that works for your family.
- Once you are together, go around and have each person share any big things that will be going on for them this week. Now, you may have to ask your teenager specific questions like "Do you have a test?"—but the goal is to have everyone share at least *one* thing that will be happening in the next seven days.

Here are some ideas if you need help getting teenagers to share: Do they have a sporting event, tryouts, finals, speech debates, a school dance, a big test, a hard conversation, a class they really hate going to, a goal they are trying to reach, something they are nervous or excited about?

Once all the family members have each identified at least one thing happening this week, ask them (or help them figure out) what time that event is going to happen and on what day.

For example: Maddie has a science test during second period (which is 9:15 a.m.) on Tuesday, and Diego has soccer tryouts after school (which is 3:45 p.m.) on Thursday.

Now, when my parents did this with Laura and me, my dad would set a timer on his watch, and my mom would write it in her Day-Timer.

Today, with iPhones, Apple Watches, Google Home, and Google Calendar, it's even easier. Just tell Siri or Alexa to remind you to "pray for [name] and their [test, tryout, conversation, and so forth] at [time] on [day]" right there at the dinner table.

As you add the reminder, tell your kids that you love them, you will be praying for them at that exact moment, and no matter the outcome, they have your blessing and you will always be crazy about them.

My parents did this with us each week. I cannot tell you the number of times I'd be sitting in class, terrified about the test the teacher was handing out, and my eyes would go to the clock. I'd instantly be reminded that my parents were praying for me at that exact moment and that, no matter what, I was coming home to a mom and dad who were proud of me.

Bonus: When your kids get home that day, *ask them* how their event went. It's a perfect opportunity to talk to them about what happened that day and how they are feeling and to give support, encouragement, or a blessing right when they need it.

2. Try Apples and Peanut Butter

The teenage years can be unpredictable, but you don't have to be.

The blessing I remember most as a teenager had to do with late-night talks over apples and peanut butter. After every dance, late-night game, or even just a night out with friends that stretched on all the way to curfew (or beyond), I knew that regardless of how the night went I'd have someone to talk to.

I would walk in the house, and my dad would be waiting for me with my favorite snack, apples and peanut butter. We'd sit at the kitchen table, and as I munched, he would ask me questions about my night.

Sometimes I'd have fun stories to share, or other nights, like the time I didn't get asked to prom or a mean guy at school called me fat, our conversations would be full of my tears. But no matter what was going on in my life, I knew there would be someone there at the end of the day who cared about what I was going through.

After I finished my snack and our conversation ended, my dad would hug me, pray for me, and give me his blessing.

Now, though I'm well into my thirties, my dad *still* waits up for me anytime I'm back in Arizona. We still sit down and talk about my night. And I still get a hug and a blessing.

These are by far some of the most meaningful and important conversations I had during my teen years, and they have turned out to be some of the most meaningful and important in my adult life as well.

It may cost you some sleep and some extra money in snacks, but it will bring you and your child more blessings than you know.

I asked my dad once if he ever wanted to go to bed instead of waiting up to talk to me. His eyes got misty, and he said, "I asked my mom that same question once, and I'm going to tell you exactly what she told me . . . 'I can always go back to sleep . . . but I won't always be here to have these talks with you. There's nothing I'd rather do than talk to you.'"

3. Write a Note

Don't underestimate the power of a note. Does your child have a paper that he started the night before it was due? Does she have a big test that she is worried about? Is he trying out for a team? Feeling jittery about prom? Nervous about what her friends will think?

Write your child a quick note!

My sister, Laura, would start her term papers weeks in advance and would get a full night's sleep the night before they were due.

I didn't even know what my topic was going to be until after dinner the night before the paper was to be turned in.

But both Laura and I got notes of encouragement slipped under our door the night before we turned in our papers.

Even my sophomore year, when my dad had to drive my friend Nicole and me to Kinko's (before it was FedEx) at 3:00 a.m. to make copies of all our sources and footnotes (this was before the days when home copiers were available, the internet was deemed credible enough to cite, and kids submitted their papers electronically). I still found a note under my door telling me I was a great writer and the Lord had gifted me to use my words.

And there was another time when I came home from cheer-leading tryouts to find small notes taped all around my room from my dad, mom, sister, and even the dog.

Again, these notes weren't long. Just one or two sentences. But I still have some of them hanging in my office and lying on my nightstand today.

4. Do Your Homework

As your kids get older, they may become less excited about things you once did together, especially as they begin to test the waters with what they feel called to do in life. But don't get discouraged! There are still some powerful ways you can bless them—it just may take some research.

What is your child into? Music? Go to a concert, just the two of you. And give your child a blessing at dinner before you go.

Basketball? Go to a game, even if you're in the nosebleed section and regardless of whether it's the local, college, or state championship team. Again, make sure to carve out some time over dinner or in the car to bless your child.

Science? Visit a museum or attend a lecture together, or line up a college visit complete with a lab experience.

Fashion? Go to a local show, watch *Project Runway*, or volunteer to help with your child's latest sewing project.

The bottom line is to meet your children where they are at. If you don't know anything about what gets them excited, do your research.

One of the best examples I've personally seen of this practice comes from my grandmother. My grandma did her homework on what each of her boys was passionate about. She could ask them questions, talk to them at length about their passions, and had written notes in the margins of many of the magazines and journals based on their conversations.

She found a way to learn about them—to meet them where they were at—and encourage them when they were struggling in life or in their careers.

Your kids may change their minds fifty times before they land where the Lord has them. But you and your kids will not feel a single minute is wasted if you take the time to learn about what they love and encourage them as they learn as well.

Blessing Adult Kids

Here are some thoughts for blessing your children who are grown.

1. Keep Using Snail Mail

Emails and texts are great, but there is something very special about a handwritten note.

Every week while Laura and I were in college, we would get a letter from home. Really, these "letters" were humorous greeting cards in which my parents would write one or two lines of encouragement before signing and sending them to us.

Often these notes would also include an article they had found that related to what we were studying, a picture, a gift card, or even (when we really needed it) some cash to help us get through the week.

I still have a box under my bed *full* of four years' worth of cards. Every single handwritten sentence from home helped make the hardest moments of college seem bearable.

2. Celebrate the First Day of Work

I'll never forget my first day at my first job out of college. You know, your first "real" job.

The night before I was set to go to work, my parents came into my room. They had a note and a small wrapped package for me. Inside was a small antique piggy bank shaped like a small metal tin.

They told me, "Kari, no matter where you work or what you do, you are always worth more to us than any paycheck." They prayed for me and said a blessing over my new season.

I *still* have that piggy bank on my desk today, and there isn't a day that goes by that I don't look at it and think about the fact that no matter what I did or didn't get done that day, I'm worth *so* much more to my parents than my achievements or failures. (Which is especially handy, since I now am blessed to work with my dad.)

3. Keep Exploring

You might assume that it doesn't matter as much to your adult children if you are interested in them and their lives, but that's actually the opposite of what they're thinking. They may not be seeking as much guidance from you as they were when they were younger, but they still want to know that you care about what's going on in their lives.

Take the game Twenty Questions from the previous section and adapt it for your adult children. For example, come up with twenty big questions (with three mini follow-up questions) that you can ask them about their work, life, interests, hobbies, and so forth. (Note: This may require some homework. See the previous section under Do Your Homework for ideas.)

For example, let's say your son works for a construction company, and you've done your homework and found out about a new development that could help with the longevity of pavement. You could ask one big question like, "I was reading the other day that a new type of asphalt has been developed that can last ten years without repaving. What are your thoughts on that?" Then you can ask three small follow-up questions like, "Do you think it would help or hurt construction companies? Is it something you would recommend to your clients? Do you think there is a better solution?"

Don't ask your children all twenty questions at once, but every week pick up the phone or grab dinner and ask a few questions . . . just to get to know them. Make sure to tell them at the end of your conversation that you love them, that you're proud of them, and that they have your blessing.

If your child is struggling or living a life that's different from what you pictured for them, try to pick questions that show your genuine care—not your disapproval of their decisions. This means that if you don't like your child's job, significant other, or personal habits, keep questions about those topics off-limits for this conversation. You can still speak truth and share your opinion during other times of conversation. However, those things will fall on deaf ears and can even cause distance in your relationship if you don't take time to *build* the relationship as well (especially if you are coming out of challenges from the teen years).

Building a relationship means getting to know your child—and letting your child get to know you in a different way. Be vulnerable with them and spend time investing in the relationship by asking questions and listening—not sharing what *you* would do unless you're asked.

So if you really don't like your child's job and can't ask questions about it without voicing your opinion or disdain, skip that topic and pick something neutral. The more your children feel free in sharing with you, the more willing they'll become to let you speak into other areas of their lives as well.

4. Commit to Weekly Video

With the exception of a few short months, I have not lived in the same state as my parents since I went to college. While we made it work during and after college, our relationship got even better with the blessing of FaceTime. There is nothing like being able to "see" your kids and for them to "see" you. It also helps cut down on misunderstandings in communication that are all too common in texting and even phone conversations. While your millennial or Gen X kid may still favor texting, try incorporating FaceTime into your blessing routine at least once a week.

Helpful hint: smile—a lot!—while you have your kids on camera. And make sure you give them your blessing before you get off the call. It says in Proverbs that bright eyes make the heart glad (Proverbs 15:30), and that counts for FaceTime too!

5. Make a Care Package

There is nothing in the world like a care package. Imagine it: you get home, and sitting on your kitchen countertop is a box that contains some of your favorite things in the whole world, including a note from your parents telling you how valuable you are to them.

In reality, it may look more like your child picking this up from an Amazon locker, and the package may have a mixture of necessities (we can always use more socks!) and fun items. But no matter what's inside, it's a great way to bless your adult child—even if they live in the same city as you.

Try to include things your child really loves—not just things that you want them to have. And don't forget a note of blessing as well!

6. Give Them a Blessing Coin

Find a special time to give a Blessing Coin to your child. A Blessing Coin is something special that we have created to help you give your blessing. These coins have the five elements of the Blessing on them and are both a great reminder for you to keep choosing to give your blessing and a great visible reminder for your child that they *have* your blessing.

To give your child the coin, schedule some time with them. Go to a game together, to dinner, to see a concert, to play racquetball, or even to shoot hoops in your front yard.

Near the end of your time together, share your blessing with your child and give them the coin. Tell your child something like this: "You are more valuable to me than any coin or any amount of money. This coin is something you can keep to remind you every day that you will *always* have my blessing."

You can find Blessing Coins at TheBlessing.com.

Blessing Your Grandkids

Before we launch into some creative and meaningful ideas for grandparents, let me (John) share with you something I remember vividly about my grandfather. We called it the Great Parakeet Fiasco, and it became a legend in our home.

I was in second grade. Our parakeet had escaped from its cage while we were at school. My grandmother was cleaning the parakeet's cage, and Tweetie (yes, we were creative in naming pets, including Mr. Cat) decided to make a break for it—and got past her hand and flew into the living room. Grandma ordered my grandfather to catch the runaway parakeet, which he did by throwing a dish towel over it and then taking it in his hand.

But then it happened. Tweetie was obviously scared and bit a large chunk out of Grandfather's right index finger. Almost spasmodically, Grandfather squeezed his hand and cried out, "Dumb bird!" (or words to that effect). My grandfather was an old carpenter and a hard-as-nails Texan. Tragically—and he truly didn't mean to—his hands were so strong, that spasmodic squeeze was all it took to send Tweetie to parakeet heaven. (Please, no emails on the theology of such a place.)

I share this tragic story not because it was funny. It wasn't. But what happened was almost as bad. My grandmother was not in the room when Tweetie expired. So my grandfather took the bird and put it back in the cage. He wrapped its feet around the wooden perch that stretched across the middle of the cage and then leaned the parakeet up against the side, hoping it would look like Tweetie had fallen asleep and passed away.

However, like any great cover-up, it didn't work. Pandemonium broke out when we got home from school, and a misshapen bird led to a reluctant confession. And here is why I share this very sad story.

There is simply no way to hide things—for long—from our

children or grandchildren. They are like God's little spies. And as God's Word says, "Nothing is concealed that will not become evident, nor anything hidden that will not be known and come to light" (Luke 8:17 NASB).

That doesn't mean we have to be perfect grandparents. None of us are or will be. But kids remember our actions—positive or negative. And as we get older and realize more acutely that there is an expiration date on all our lives, it's important we realize that our children and grandchildren won't remember all the places we took them, but they will remember how we loved them.

So here are several small ways to bring the Blessing home to a grandchild's life.

1. Team Up with Grandchildren

First, real adults do chores. And hopefully, your grandchildren will have parents who are wise enough to assign them some. If they're too young to do them, that's when kids want to do chores! But if they're old enough to do the chore, odds are they aren't going to like it.

Which is where you step in—not to do the chore for them, but with them. And while you're doing that task, talk to them about some chores you had to do as a child: the fun ones, the challenging ones. The time you got caught skipping out on a chore—and the consequences—or the thing that chore actually taught you. Your chores will very likely show you grew up in a very different world from today and your grandchildren's chores. And this will give you a chance to share your story—which is in itself a wonderful way of blessing each of your grandchildren.

I'm grateful for the stories that my mother told me about the pigs down in the mud and how they knew it was her when she was trying to feed them. Or my grandfather talking about falling asleep while driving the tractor and waking up when it ran into—and through—the neighbors' fence. It was another world. It brought me closer to both of them to hear about their chores and challenges, and it remains a blessing to me to this day.

2. Anything-Goes Dinner Holiday

You might talk with your children before the next time you're watching the grandkids to ask their permission to do this. (Or you can ask for forgiveness!) But one great way to bless kids is to declare a national holiday on whatever day you've got the kids for dinner. Announce it as National Anything-Goes Dinner Night and then head to the store. There, you let *them* pick out a main course, a something-else side to put on their plate, and a dessert. And since it's anything goes, get ready for chocolate milk for the main course, peanut butter mixed with jelly as their side, and macaroni and cheese for their dessert.

While they're eating, talk to them about how different things can still be good together—like how their grandmother and grandfather are different and the Lord has made them a wonderful mix. And how their mother and father are very different from each other, but they're wonderful together too. And, finally, how that grandson in front of you and the granddaughter on the other side of the table are very different from each other—but they're very loved as well. That's the message of 1 Corinthians 12. We're not all "eyes." We're not all "ears." But we are all placed in the body right where we belong.

It's a fun way to point out what you love about them—and how you can love someone (like their sister) just as much, even though you are very different from that person. This even provides a great opportunity to talk to your grandchildren about racial differences and help ensure that our next generation will step up and heal racial division and hurts in our country as well.

3. Teach That God Is Always There

Kids grow up in a flash. But even so, our time as grandparents is ticking on an even faster clock. One way to leave your grandchildren a picture of how your love and God's love will always be there—even when they can't see it—is to bring some balloons to the dinner table.

Make sure there's no choking hazard for little kids. With older kids, while still supervising them, have them each hold and blow up a balloon. Then, rather than having them tie the balloon, tell them instead to aim it at their grandmother (wherever she's sitting) or grandfather and "shoot" the balloon at them! Kids love watching those balloons shoot across the room! Let them do it several times until they're all blown out.

Then say, "Kids, let me ask you a question. Can you see air?" And of course, unless you live in Southern California, the answer for most kids will be no. Then share with them about what they've been doing with their balloons. "Did you know that air—even if you can't see it—has power? Just like how that balloon shot across the room. And air, even if you can't see it, is a part of space, just like the way air shapes a balloon when you blow into it."

Then tell them, "I want you kids to remember something, and

that's the answer to a question. 'Is God real—even though you can't see him?'" They may say yes, or they may say no. But you can tell them, "Kids, just like air—God is there." You might even want to read them Colossians 1:15: "Christ is the visible expression of the invisible God" (PHILLIPS). "We can't see God the Father—but we got to see Jesus. And now, even though Jesus has gone back up to heaven, he is still real. And still here through the Holy Spirit."

Next, you could also tell them what my grandmother told me. "John, the day will come when I'm not here and I'm up in heaven with Jesus." (She was dying of pancreatic cancer, and I was eight years old.) "Just because you can't see something, like Jesus or heaven, or my love when I'm up in heaven—they're all real."

4. Read Them Their Own Hero's Journey

Here's a last suggestion on something small you can do with a child who needs some attention and has some time for you to read to them (think about *The Princess Bride* and reading to a not super-sick but still stuck-at-home kid). Read your grandchild a book (and if you can, purchase it as a gift) that has a pronounced hero or heroine in it. But each time that character's name comes up in the book, change that character's name to your grandchild's name.

Take the Chronicles of Narnia. The second book in that wonderful children's series is *The Lion, the Witch and the Wardrobe.* (You can get it online for only a few dollars.) Let's say you have a granddaughter. In that book, Lucy is not only a main character but is very smart and brave. And so, too, will be your granddaughter (let's call her Heather). As you read, every time Lucy's name appears in the book, point to your granddaughter and substitute Heather for Lucy.

It's Heather who meets Mr. Beaver. It's Heather who runs from the White Witch. It's Heather who meets Aslan the great lion. It's a small way to say to a grandchild, "I see something special inside of you." And forever that book can be something on her shelf that makes her say, "My grandmother read me that book. And she thought I was as brave and kind as Lucy."

5. Don't Forget *Your* Kids

Sometimes it's much easier to bless our grandkids than it is to bless our own kids. This is especially true in relationships with our adult kids where there may be layers of hurt or emotional distance.

However, by forgetting to bless our own children, we can inadvertently cause pain in that relationship and drive a wedge between us and them. Or we create a much bigger wedge—or, in some cases, a Grand Canyon–size hole.

So no matter how much fun you are having with your grandkids, don't forget their parents! Go back through this list and make sure that you are still taking time to bless your kids—just as much time as you spend blessing your grandchildren.

No matter what age or stage of life, we *all* need to know that we have the Blessing. Especially from our parents.

Okay, you've just read nearly thirty different ways you can give the blessing to your kids and grandkids today! That's pretty amazing.

But while we encourage you to steal and use every single one of those ideas, we also want you to get comfortable with creating your own.

Blessing Activity

Write down one blessing idea that stood out to you in this chapter. If you have more than one kid or grandkid, make sure to write down one idea for each of them.

Next, pick a time this upcoming week when you can do this blessing idea with your child or grandchild. Again, if you have more than one, take the time to do these separately with each of them one-on-one. Don't forget to add it to your reminders or calendar so you don't forget!

Blessing for _____

Day: _____ Time: _____

Blessing Idea: _____

Blessing for _____

Day: _____ Time: _____

Blessing Idea: _____

Blessing for _____

Day: _____ Time: _____

Blessing Idea: _____

Blessing for _____

Day: _____ Time: _____

Blessing Idea: _____

Making the Blessing a Lifestyle

Okay, it's time to come up with some of your own ideas to bless your kids and grandkids. The categories below are a great way to get started.

You don't need to fill out all of these, but you can use them as a guideline to get your ideas flowing.

Try to come up with at least three ideas *total* for blessing *each* kid. Add them to your calendar—one a week for three weeks—so you'll have three weeks of blessing your kids ready to go! *Note: You can also go to TheBlessing.com to create a blessing plan for your kids.*

1. What are some activities/hobbies/passions that your child enjoys? (e.g., cars, football, reading, running, painting)

2. What are some things you have done in the past that your child has really enjoyed? (e.g., time talking, throwing the baseball, making dinner together, eating a special snack)

3. What are some big things that your child has coming up in the next few months? (e.g., a birthday, a report due at school, a driver's test, college applications)

4. What are some things that you really love and appreciate about your child? (e.g., are really caring, a great big brother or sister, super funny, full of positivity)

5. What are some things that your child is struggling with? (e.g., Is your child having a hard time with a teacher at school? Is math really a struggle? Is that one friend leaving them out? Has the school bully made your child a target?)

6. What is something tangible that your child really likes (such as their favorite food, drink, or way to celebrate)?

7. Other:

Making the Blessing a Lifestyle

Now look at the three things you've written in each category.

Next to each item, brainstorm and write down at least one way you can turn each idea into a blessing.

Finally, take each of the blessing ideas you've written and add them to your reminders or calendar. Do one a week for three weeks.

More Resources

For more ideas on coming up with blessings for your kids, grandkids, or other relationships that matter most to you, head to StrongFamilies.com and check out our resources, podcast, social media, or blog.

CHAPTER 12

Blessing Your Spouse

Another relationship that requires your blessing is your marriage. Blessing your spouse is just as important as blessing your kids. We've literally seen it change and repair thousands of relationships.

It's also hugely important for your kids to see. What we model matters. Modeling the Blessing in your marriage is a great way not only to help your kids feel happier and more secure in your home but also to set them up for success in their future relationships.

While planning a special event to give your spouse your blessing is a great idea and something you should do, the goal is to make giving your blessing an ongoing part of your marriage, not just a onetime action. To help take the stress out of this for you, we have tons of ready-to-use examples right here in this chapter.

Just as in the previous chapter, many of these ideas are things that my husband, Joey, and I (Kari) have done or that I've seen my parents or close friends model. Joey and I do *not* have a perfect marriage. There are a million things that we need to work on (999,999 are mine) and at least as many ways where we fall short. However, these are ideas that we've tried, learned from, or have seen work.[1]

---

1. If you are looking for additional ways to strengthen your marriage, my book *The Merge for Marriage* has practical and helpful ways to bless and grow closer together. You can find the book and learn more at KariTrent.com or StrongFamilies.com.

Practical Ideas

Okay, let's jump into some ways to make the Blessing a key, ongoing part of your marriage.

1. Create a Blessing Jar

Get two mason jars. Put your name on one and your spouse's name on the other. Then cut two sheets of paper into forty small strips (twenty strips per sheet of paper).

You and your spouse each get twenty strips. Now write down twenty ways that your spouse can bless you, and have your spouse do the same.

For example, some of the ideas in my jar are to spend a night together without our cell phones, play a board game with me, bring me flowers, and hang up the curtain rods in the guest bedroom and office.

Some of the ideas in Joey's jar are to have chips and salsa for me when I get home, plan and make dinner, help me work in the yard, and take a drive with me in the truck.

Once a week, pick a strip of paper out of your spouse's jar and do what it says. Joey and I pick a random day that works for us (and we often pick different days).

If you take time to do this, you now have twenty weeks of blessings—things your spouse has said would bless them—that you can do! You can also add more blessing ideas as you think of them.

There is just one rule: you can't use any negatives. Meaning, you can't write things like "Take the trash out for me, for once in your life" or "Plan a date night . . . if you even care about me at all."

Similarly, when you actually go to complete the blessing you've picked out of your spouse's jar, you can't throw it back at your spouse in a negative way either, like, "See, I do listen to you!" or "Of course, you would choose something that I don't like."

The goal is to *bless* your spouse in a way that means something to them—without questions, comments, or snide remarks.

2. Leave a Note

Are you leaving for a trip? Does your spouse have a big day at work? Maybe a difficult meeting or conversation is on the horizon? Is your spouse about to complete a long run or a personal challenge? Write your spouse a blessing note and leave it somewhere fun for them to discover.

We've been doing this for four years now, so you'd think I'd be ready. However, last night, as Joey was getting ready to leave for a work trip, I felt overwhelmed. Joey left at 4:00 a.m. for the airport, and by the time I rolled out of bed, I was feeling even more overwhelmed. So I did what any woman facing a crisis would do . . . I headed right to the coffee maker. My scowl immediately turned into a smile, and then into tears, as I saw a note in a coffee mug from Joey. He told me he loved me, he missed me already, and that we were not only going to get through this season but come out stronger and closer together. He also promised me a date night when he got home on Sunday (something from my jar that blesses me a lot).

To add to the blessing, he had also made me coffee and put it in a thermos right next to the coffee cup. Talk about husband of the year!

What do you and your spouse have coming up where they could use some encouragement? Leave a note in her lunch, put it in his car for him to find in the morning, hide it inside her running shoe, or set it in his coffee mug (just don't forget the coffee!).

3. Share a Nightly Blessing

We've mentioned giving your kids a bedtime blessing, but did you know you can do that with your spouse as well? In fact, we recommend it!

Every night, as Joey and I go to bed, we give each other a blessing. As we lie down, I'll turn to him and ask, "Why do you love me today?" and Joey will answer with one reason (or often more than one reason) why he loves and appreciates me, along with something specific I did that day that blessed him. Then Joey will ask me, "Why do you love me today?" and I'll respond with one or more things that I love about Joey and one way that he blessed me that day.

There is only one rule: you *have* to answer, and it *has* to be positive.

Now, you may think this is silly and not something you would ever do. That's okay. However, I would encourage you to see the bigger picture:

- It's a great way to end the day. No matter how many dis-agreements you and your spouse have gotten into or how frustrated one of you is, taking a few minutes to think through the day and identify the *good*—the blessings have the power to change your mindsets.

- Love is active. Hearing "I love you" is great, but being given a specific reason why you are still loved, wanted, and valued *today* is something we all need.
- Saying thanks is important—really! Studies have shown, again and again, that saying thanks reinforces *and* strengthens relationships.

So if you follow our bedtime blessing formula—*one reason you love them + one way they blessed you today + thank you, that really blessed me*—you will encourage your spouse, strengthen your relationship, change your mindset from negative to positive (or emphasize the positive), and reinforce the behavior you'd like to see more of, all in one sentence!

Talk about a win!

4. Touch

Just as touch is an important part of blessing your kids, it's just as important in blessing your spouse.

You don't need to violate PDA rules or make your kids groan in disgust unless you want to (and let's be honest, that's one of the best parts of being a parent!). However, you do need to keep touch a key part of your marriage.

Hold her hand, give him a quick shoulder rub, hug her when she comes in the door, put your arm around him during the movie, cuddle up while you lie in bed and share your bedtime blessing, dance together in the kitchen, put your hand on his shoulder in encouragement, kiss her. Even a high-five is a powerful way to build touch and attachment in your marriage.

One argument we get from readers about this is "I don't feel very affectionate." While this may be true, studies show that physical touch can actually lead you to experience affection.[1] As my dad always says, "Actions dictate feelings . . . not the reverse," meaning, if you do it, you will begin to feel it. But if you wait to feel like doing it before you start, you may never start at all.

Appropriate meaningful touch doesn't just need to be done when you're alone. It's actually really great for your kids to see as well. Not only does it show them how to model it in their own lives,[2] but studies have shown that parents who demonstrate appropriate meaningful touch in front of their kids actually make their kids feel more confident and secure about their parents' marriage—and their homelife as well.[3] It literally makes them feel like they are part of a happier home!

So you are not only blessing your spouse but also blessing your kids and setting them up for success in their future relationships.

5. Give a "Just Because" Gift

It doesn't have to be your spouse's birthday or a holiday to give them a gift. The key to this present is to get your spouse something they have mentioned or been wanting "just because."

Now, before you head off to the store to buy whatever just popped into your head, let me tell you how to make sure your spouse will see it as a blessing. Trust me, you will thank me later.

Joey, being the kind, amazing, wonderful, awesome husband that he is, decided to try this one day. We have been remodeling our house ourselves. Having no real idea of what we were getting into, our remodel has become more of a "demolish and leave it" situation instead of the DIY magic that Chip and Joanna Gaines so elegantly modeled on *Fixer Upper* . . . but that's another story. While there are a million things unfinished—including floors, ceilings, and one very persistent roof leak, the one thing that I had been begging Joey to get were new outlet and light switch covers. The ones that we had were either old, broken, discolored, or missing, which made turning on the lights or plugging something in both a challenge and a potential fire hazard.

So, on a bright fall day, Joey came in the door bursting with excitement, holding a beautifully gift-wrapped box with a large gold bow on top. Grinning with joy, I opened it excitedly only to find . . . outlet and light switch covers inside.

Now, I was determined not to storm out of the room or tell Joey that he clearly didn't understand how to give a gift—and I'm really glad I didn't. Because at that moment, he handed me a note.

The note said, "Kari, you are so full of energy and electricity that you power up our entire family. You add light to people who need it, and you light up my life as well. Love, Joey."

Y'all, my jaw dropped, and yes . . . I cried. Looking back on that moment, I really believe that a disaster was averted by the note.

Now some of you may be thinking, *I don't get it. Didn't you want the outlet and light switch covers?* Yes. Yes, I did. However, what I wanted more was for Joey to get me something that made me feel loved, which is why I was initially disappointed with the gift when I opened it.

My disappointment immediately turned to joy when I realized that Joey didn't just see the outlet and light switch covers at Home Depot and bring them home but that he specifically saw something special in me at the same time. In fact, every time I look at our new, beautiful, matching, clean outlet and light switch covers, I'm reminded that my husband thinks I power up our family and add light to his life. I'm pretty sure that word picture Joey used will stay with me every single day we live in this house.

If you need extra help coming up with a word picture that will bless your spouse, we have an entire book called *The Language of Love* that will walk you through creating your own word pictures step-by-step. You can also check out our website, podcast, and social media for more tips on using word pictures in your relationships as well.

6. Do Your Spouse's Chores

I don't know how chores work in your home, but in ours, we often end up doing the same tasks each week to keep the house clean. Joey cleans the bathrooms, and I dust and vacuum.

One surefire way we've found to bless each other is by doing the other person's chores. Typically it looks like this: If Joey is out of town for work, I will clean the bathrooms as well as dust and vacuum. That way, when he gets home, we can relax together and spend time connecting—instead of working.

Joey has done this for me as well. He will dust and vacuum as well as clean the bathrooms. He's even gone so far as to have a romantic dinner waiting for me when I got home from the airport. No small feat with busy schedules and two small boys.

There is nothing like coming home to a clean house and an amazing meal and an evening full of time and joy with your spouse and your kids if they are still up. Not to mention that this is a super practical way to bless your spouse if they are busy with work, tired from a long week, or pitching in to help with something extra with the kids.

Give it a try! And add a note or meal to your blessing as well for an added wow.

7. Give Your Spouse a Kid-Free Night

Does your spouse look a little tired? Try blessing them with a kid-free night. We all love our kids, but sometimes we need time to ourselves to recharge.

A kid-free night can look any way your spouse wants it to: A night alone to read, take a bath, and relax. A night out with a good friend or to take a class. Or even just a night to have a bowl of popcorn and sole possession of the DVR.

The goal is to give your spouse a night off. You and the kids can go to Grandma's for the night. Or you can save up and give your spouse a night at a local hotel (a lot of hotels have great deals in the offseason).

As you can see, there are tons of ways that you can live out the Blessing each day with your spouse.

Blessing Activity

What are three ways that your spouse wants to be blessed? (If you don't know, ask your spouse!) Now, write down one blessing that you are going to give your spouse each week for the next five weeks. Add a date and time to it and put it in your phone or calendar to remind you.

Week 1:	
Week 2:	
Week 3:	
Week 4:	
Week 5:	

Making the Blessing a Lifestyle

Okay, it's time to come up with some of your own ideas to bless your spouse. The categories below are a great way to get started.

You don't need to fill out all of these, but you can use them as a guideline to get you started.

Try to come up with at least three ideas *total* for blessing your spouse.

Add them to your calendar—one blessing a week for three weeks—so you'll have three weeks of blessing your spouse ready to go! *Note: You can also go to TheBlessing.com/blessingplan to come up with a personalized, yearlong plan to bless your spouse in ways that are important to them.*

1. What are some activities/hobbies/passions that your spouse enjoys? (e.g., cars, football, reading, running, painting)

2. What are some things you have done in the past that have blessed your spouse? (e.g., made dinner, cleaned the garage, filled up the gas tank, washed the car)

3. What are some big things that your spouse has coming up in the next few months? (e.g., a birthday, a presentation at work, a run, a tough day—like the anniversary of a parent's death)

4. What are some things that you really love and appreciate about your spouse? (e.g., my spouse is really caring, good with the budget, a hard worker, funny, full of positivity)

5. What are some things that your spouse is struggling with? (e.g., Are they feeling discouraged about what's going on at work? Are they struggling to connect with one of your kids? Does your spouse feel like they need to add in some healthy habits but can't seem to find the time?)

6. What is something tangible that your spouse really likes (such as their favorite food, drink, or way to celebrate)?

7. Other:

Now look at the three things you've written in each category.

Next to each item, brainstorm and write down at least one way that you can turn each idea into a blessing.

Finally, take each of the blessing ideas you've written and add them to your reminders or calendar. Do one blessing a week for three weeks.

CHAPTER 13

Blessing When You're Single

When it comes to our calling to bless others, without hesitation, so much of this book applies to singles, like blessing your parents, living out the five elements of the Blessing, or bringing the Blessing home to roommates or those at work who need it.

But in this chapter I'd like to focus on two areas where singles can be world-class in blessing others. And the first is in applying the Blessing with your siblings.

Blessing Your Siblings

When it comes to the Blessing, if there is one relationship that we can tend to overlook—or even take for granted—it's the relationship we have with a sibling. For my dad and I (Kari), the Blessing always starts at home, and it's no different here. There is something about a brother or a sister that can bring out the best in us—and also the absolute worst.

We see and hear about this all the time in families: "My brother and I are just so different." "My sister and I fight all the time." "We are family, but we aren't friends."

Hopefully, you and your sibling grew up in a home where you received the Blessing. If that wasn't the case, it's not all on you to try and make up for a parent's lack of the Blessing. But what you can do is give your sibling a tremendous gift—*your* blessing.

The reality is your sibling(s) will always be your family. They should be your biggest advocate, and you should be theirs. While this may not be the current reality in your relationship, the good news is, no matter where your relationship is today, it's never too late to start giving them your blessing. It just may be the tipping point that can lead to a breakthrough in your differences—and the creation of a deep and lifelong friendship.

So what are some ways that you can start blessing your sibling(s)?

1. Don't Hold Back

One thing I've noticed with my sister, Laura, and me is that we tend to hold back on saying positive things because we are family. I know she's always going to be there—so I tend to just assume that she knows how much I love her and how proud I am of her.

But just like we've shared in the rest of this book, if we don't say it, people don't know it. And even when it comes to our siblings, we can't just assume. In fact, when I started to change my perception about intentionally blessing Laura, our relationship changed. We got closer, spent more time together, and even developed a deep friendship—one that goes beyond "just family."

So how can you start using words to bless your brother or sister? Start by challenging yourself to never miss an opportunity to "say something."

Did you see something today that reminded you of them? Text them a picture—with a quick blessing attached. Did they bring an amazing dish to the family picnic? Thank them for doing that—and add a quick blessing. Your blessing doesn't need to be about food, but use it as an on-ramp to share about something positive you see in them.

Did they get a promotion at work? Send them a gift card, take them to dinner, or find another activity they enjoy and celebrate with them.

Whether you live close to your siblings or far away, there are a million ways that you can choose to step toward them. They don't need to be grand gestures. You just need to start—and keep making that choice.

2. Remember Important Days

Another way you can bless your siblings is to remember days that are important to them.

Is New Year's a big day for them? Send them a blessing. Is their birthday or anniversary coming up? Send them a blessing. Do they have a big interview or presentation this week? Send them a blessing.

The best way I've found to do this is to put big-days-for-Laura in my phone. I even set a reminder a week before if I need to send her a gift or a card. That way on the big day she knows she has my blessing.

For your siblings, it may be that their birthdays or their kids' birthdays are a huge deal. Or maybe it's work- or school-related. Or perhaps it's a date that reminds them of the loss of a loved one. Whatever the dates are, planning and figuring out what days are important to them can take work. But it is worth every second.

When you show up physically or emotionally on a day when they need you, it can make all the difference in the world in your relationship as well.

So stop and take a few minutes to write down some important dates that matter to your siblings. Put them in your phone—with reminders ahead of time if you need to. Don't forget to send them a blessing when you get that reminder in the weeks and months ahead.

3. Speak Their Language

One thing we see again and again with siblings is that we often try to bless them the same way we would want to be blessed. And we are shocked, offended, and angry when they don't feel blessed by it.

So when you go to bless your siblings, you need to make sure you are speaking their language.

Do they want to talk over coffee or a meal instead of seeing the latest *Star Wars* film? Do they feel blessed when you fill up their gas tank or help them with a project? Do they light up when they talk about cars, woodworking, photography, horses, running, or another hobby?

Whatever it is that blesses them, do that. Just don't forget to find time to give them your blessing as well.

It can feel uncomfortable when you break out of the norm and meet someone where they are at. You may not even enjoy the hobby, movie, or activity that you do with them. However, this isn't for you. It's for them. You are doing this to step toward them, to support them, to show them that you love them, and to bless them in a way that means something to them. So feel free to have an uncomfortable or less-than-ideal afternoon. Just keep in mind that whatever you lose in time or enjoyment, you will gain back exponentially in the relationship.

4. Be Consistent

Your relationships with your siblings will most likely be the longest ones you will ever have. You'll know them longer than your spouse, they will most likely outlive your parents, and they will still be your siblings when friendships come and go.

That said, the key to keeping the Blessing a part of your longest-running relationships is to be consistent. This is especially important if you have tension in a relationship or don't have a strong friendship yet. Consistency is key and is a major thing your brother or sister will be looking for as you go. So how can you build blessing consistency into your relationship with your siblings?

One way is to start small. It can be really temping to go "all out" and try to do big gestures and lots of blessings at once. However, the key to consistent change is to make small, two-degree changes. Then, after you've mastered one two-degree change, you can add another two-degree change, and so on. While this may not seem as exciting or appear on the surface to be as effective, it works.

But let's come up with one small, two-degree action you can do right now to bless your brother or sister. For me, I'm going to call Laura once a week for the next month. Even if it's a five-minute call, I'm going to choose to pick up the phone and not hang up until I've given her my blessing. That's it! One small, two-degree thing that I can do consistently. Next month, I can add to that with another small thing. But for this month, all I'm going to do is pick up the phone and bless her once a week.

Okay, now it's your turn. What is one small thing that you can do consistently to bless your siblings this month? Write it down, add it to your calendar, and take action. It's a great and easy way to build consistency when it comes to blessing.

Blessing Your Friends

We all have that one friend who is just the *best* at blessing others. You know who I'm talking about. The one who shows up with a home-cooked meal, your favorite movie, and their healing essential oil blend—just because you "sounded stuffy" on the phone.

Or the friend who seems to notice any person who needs a ride to the airport or could use help moving, volunteers for everything, and at the same time is able to make an award–winning homemade dessert for your weekly small group.

I am not that friend.

In fact, it has taken a lot of time, work, effort, and, quite frankly, failure to learn how to be even a fraction of that for those in my life. However, one thing I have realized is that the more I just take the time to be there for people—no matter what that looks like—the better my friendships and relationships become.

This section is *not* designed to make you feel like you need to be Superhero Best-Friend Bob or Superhero Best-Friend Betty. But it *is* designed to help you discover some areas where you can take the time to be there and bless those you love. After all, in my home, and probably yours as well, friends are family.

1. Look for Opportunities

While looking for opportunities to bless may sound like a simple thing, it can actually be pretty challenging. It requires us to be present, aware, and observe what's going on with our friends. It also requires us to listen to what they are saying and turn it into action. However, if we are able to do this, we can come up with some of the most meaningful and timely blessings imaginable.

Did your friend have a bad week? Bring him his favorite coffee or snack. Did your friend just get her dream job? Take her to her favorite restaurant to celebrate. Did your friend's car just get totaled? Offer to pick him up or take him to work.

There's no limit to the options, or the needs, that are out there. The key is making the time to take action. It's a choice. And we can all choose to step toward our friends, especially when they need our blessing.

2. Text Them

One thing that has helped me immensely in blessing my friends is to stop the second the Lord puts a friend on my heart or the second I think about someone and then text or call that person.

If I wait or assume I will do it later, I often get busy with life, and I forget. Not because I don't love my friends or don't want to bless them. But I'm forgetful, busy, and, as I shared, still very far from being Superhero Best-Friend Betty. So my secret is to text or call the moment I think about it. It's also been amazing to watch how the Lord has used some texts to bless a friend at key times that I had no idea about.

Ready to take action? Put down the book; write down a blessing, encouragement, prayer, or truth; and share it with the first friend who comes to your mind. Repeat as often as you can!

3. Don't Forget the Holidays

For a lot of people, the holidays can seem very far from "the most wonderful time of the year."

Some people are dealing with loss, others with broken families, and still others with not being able to fly home and be with their families for Thanksgiving or Christmas.

But the holidays create an amazing opportunity for blessing.

Every year, as far back as I can remember, my parents would spend the entire months of November and December asking each of their friends, and even acquaintances, what they were doing for the holidays. My parents would then invite them to come to our house for Thanksgiving and Christmas and celebrate with our family. It was always shocking how many people they had asked who had no plans and no holiday invitations for those two important days.

One year we had twenty people—none of them immediate family—over for Thanksgiving. Another year we had only two. The number was never important. What was important was that each person knew we wanted them there. That each person knew they were important. And, yes, that each person knew they had our blessing (something we do around the table at Thanksgiving, Christmas, and even the Fourth of July).

This tradition of blessing has led to incredible friendships and even healing for some who were mourning the loss of loved ones or broken relationships at home.

4. Take Action

In my twenties I had the incredible blessing of getting to live with two amazing families. These families not only changed my life but also taught me what it looked like to take action with blessing.

My first lesson in blessing came two days after I moved in with the Narciso family. At the time, Adam and Jenny had two amazing daughters; one was three and the other was only six months old.

Both girls were incredibly cute, sweet, and amazing. They also required a ton of love, care, energy, and support.

Being a single girl in my mid-twenties, I hadn't spent a lot of time around kids, other than during my babysitting days in high school. And being fresh out of college, I certainly hadn't lived in a house with kids since I was a kid myself.

So I was understandably surprised when I realized that the sweet little six-month-old never slept through the night. Some nights she would cry for a few hours at a time. Other times she would cry through the entire night—only to fall asleep at 6:00 a.m.—the exact time that the three-year-old would wake up!

But every morning, Jenny would get up with the girls, make breakfast, and spend the rest of her day caring for them—all while functioning on little to no sleep. The most amazing part to me was how kind, loving, and positive she was about it.

However, it was evident that she was exhausted. Adam would come home and help—but by the end of the day, they were both worn out and knew that in a few hours they would both be up again trying to get their baby back to sleep for the night.

So what does this have to do with blessing? Everything.

I began to notice there were things that I could do—without Jenny having to ask me—that would help her.

I would do the dishes after she cooked for the girls. I would clean up the table or sweep the floor after a particularly messy meal. I would offer to bring her coffee, groceries, or a treat if I was going somewhere.

While I wasn't perfect at it, and at times, I know I could have done more, I realized that I didn't need to wait for someone to ask me to help. I could see a need, meet that need, and turn it into a blessing.

Do you know of a mom who isn't getting enough sleep? Offer to babysit and give her an afternoon off. Do you know of a married couple who could really use a date night? Offer to babysit for free. Is your mom's gas tank half full after you borrowed the car? Fill it up for her. Does your roommate normally take out the trash? Do it for him as a blessing.

Remember, it's not about someone noticing or about getting a thank-you afterward. It's about blessing people where they are and in ways they need someone to show up for them. Siblings and friendships are just a few of the relationships where you can choose to live out the Blessing. For an extra bonus, leave them a little note of blessing as well.

Blessing Activity

In the space below, write down the name of each of your siblings as well as one friend who you know could use the

Blessing this week. Next to their names, write down one way that you can bless them this week. Add a date and time to it and put it in your phone or calendar to remind you. If you aren't sure what will bless your siblings, the following section will help.

Blessing for _____

Day: _____ Time: _____

Blessing Idea: _____

Making the Blessing a Lifestyle

Okay, it's time to come up with some of your own ideas to bless your siblings and your friends. Earlier in this chapter we talked about "speaking their language" when it comes to blessing, and these categories below are a great way to get started doing just that.

Fill in as many blanks as you can for your siblings, and even for your friends. Use this as a cheat sheet for coming up with blessings that are unique to that person.

If you don't know the answers, don't be afraid to ask. Do some research. It will make a big difference in your relationships if you do.

Don't forget, after you come up with your ideas, add them to your calendar—one blessing a week, for three weeks, so you'll have three weeks of blessings ready to go! This is another great two-degree tip for consistency with blessing.

1. What are some activities/hobbies/passions that they enjoy? (e.g., cars, football, reading, running, painting, dancing, horses)

2. What are some things you have done in the past that have blessed them? (e.g., made dinner, remembered a birthday, celebrated a victory, washed their car, did the dishes)

3. What are some big things that they have coming up in the next few months? (e.g., a birthday, a presentation at work, a run, a tough day—like the anniversary of a parent's death)

4. What are some things that you really love and appreciate about them? (e.g., they are really loyal, the first to celebrate others, great at solving problems)

5. What are some things that they are struggling with right now? (e.g., Are they feeling discouraged about what's going on at work? Are they struggling with a friendship or a relationship? Do they feel like their job is a dead end and they have to start over?)

6. What is something tangible that they really like (such as their favorite food, drink, or way to celebrate)?

7.   Other:

Okay, now look back over your list, and put a star next to three items.

Next to each item with a star, brainstorm and write down at least one way that you can turn each of those ideas into a blessing.

Finally, take each of the blessing ideas you've written above and add them to your reminders or calendar. Do one blessing a week for three weeks.

If you want even more ideas on how to bless your siblings or friends, check out TheBlessing.com, our podcast, or find us on social media. Don't forget to share your ideas with us as you try these and live out the Blessing at home.

Now that you've learned how to bless your siblings and your friends, it's time to live the Blessing in another important relationship—with your parents.

CHAPTER 14

Blessing Your Parents

For many of us, blessing our parents is not something we are used to doing. Not to mention that if we grew up in a home where our parents didn't give us their blessing, it can be downright uncomfortable.

However, whether your parents blessed you or chose to withhold their blessing, you can make the choice to step toward them—not out of codependency or guilt but because once you have received God's blessing, you can choose to give it to others.

Keep in mind that when you give your blessing, it may or may not be reciprocated, so keep your expectations with Jesus, not on their response. Regardless of the response of others, we are still called to "untie the knot" in forgiveness, choose to step toward them, and love them like Jesus.

As you are reading, if you find that this chapter is particularly challenging for you, we'd encourage you to get some additional support. Join one of our Blessing Groups at StrongFamilies.com, meet with a Blessing Coach, find a great counselor, or share and process with your spouse or a close friend. It's okay if this chapter is hard or brings up the fact that you may not have received your parents' blessing. But you can keep choosing to move toward life by continuing to bless others, including your parents.

One other thing to keep in mind is this: many of us tend to be closer to or relate more easily to one of our parents. We'd encourage you, if you can, to make sure you are choosing to bless both parents, even if you don't feel as connected to one as you do to the other. You can even add stepparents, in-laws, and bonus parents to this as well.

Practical Ideas

Let's jump in. Here are some simple ways that you can begin to add the Blessing into your relationship with your parents.

1. Say Thank You

You would be surprised how seldom parents hear these two super small but very important words. The truth is a simple thank-you really says a lot. And taking the time to thank your parents, even for something small, is an open door to begin to forgive (if that's needed in your relationship) and to bless in bigger ways.

You can pick something small, like, "Thank you for picking up my kids today" or "Thank you for wiping the counter for me." And then you can work your way up to bigger and more personal things as you feel comfortable.

The goal is to practice saying it . . . for as many reasons as you can think of. Make it a personal goal not to let any good thing go unthanked when it comes to your parents.

2. Write to Them

Whether it's a note, a list, a long letter, or even a book, take some time to verbalize your blessing to your parents and write it down for them.

For example, when I turned thirty, I wanted to do something to bless my mom. I was not an easy child to raise, and I put my parents through the wringer in more than one scenario.

This led to tension, specifically with my mom, for most of my teenage years and well into my twenties. As a newer Christian, and as someone who was really trying to live out the Blessing, I decided to do something to thank her and let her know that I wanted her to continue to speak into my life.

So, for a few months before my thirtieth birthday, I worked hard on a book for her. The end product was my first book, *You Were Right*. Inside the book was a list of literally everything I could think of that my mom had been right about for the past thirty years. And, y'all, I hate to admit it, but there were *a lot* of things my mom was right about.

The day of my thirtieth birthday rolled around. Joey, knowing that I had written this book, had surprised me with a flight home so I could be with my parents. I nervously handed my mom a printed copy of the book and began to read it to her out loud. My heart swelled with joy as I watched her cry happy tears over a gift I'd given her.

It was worth every second—and even a few of the mistakes it took to get me to that point in my life.

Now, before you think, *Okay, there's no way I'm going to write a book. I don't even know where to start*, don't worry! While a book is great, the reality is a simple note can have just as powerful an effect. As my mom always says, "A little note goes a *long* way." The key is to start.

3. Offer to Help

For my mom, there is no greater way to bless her than to help her around the house. It may be unloading the dishwasher, watering the plants, dusting, vacuuming, or any of the other millions of chores that I used to do in high school, but if I offer to help her—and if I actually complete the task, without any hint of my old whiny high school self—she feels like she's won the lottery.

For my dad, it's all about time with him. If he's going to run an errand or walk the dogs, I offer to go. That way, not only do we get some time together but *he* feels like he's won the Blessing lottery.

While the kid-mode part of me would rather lie on the couch and enjoy a few days off from adulting while my parents watch the grandkids, I have never regretted the time I've taken to bless my parents. And we've had some of our best conversations and biggest moments of blessing in our relationships during those times as well.

4. Share and Ask for Their Thoughts

I'm not talking about sharing something material, although you can do that too. I'm talking about sharing something emotional.

Now, in relationships where this isn't safe, skip this suggestion. But for most of us, we can choose to share more than we do currently in our relationships with our parents. The best part is, we get to choose the topic and what we share.

Once you have your situation, bring it up with your parents. Tell them what's going on, and follow that by asking, "What do you think about that?" or "What would you do in that situation?"

The first time you do this, your parents may be so shocked you are asking for their opinion that they may not know what to say. That's okay! The next week find a new situation and keep asking. Let them know that you really do want their input.

Now, there is only one rule: when they give you their input, even if it is the polar opposite of what you would actually do, thank them.

This does *not* mean that you need to do what they said. And by no means should you lie and tell them you are going to do what they suggested if you aren't. You are an adult, and it's okay to feel the way you do and take any action you choose. *But . . .* they just shared a part of their heart with you—so thank them for choosing to do that and for choosing to invest in you in that way.

If you repeat this scenario again and again, in most cases you will see some pretty amazing changes in your ability to relate, respect, and communicate with each other.

5. Don't Get Annoyed

Many of us have a standard way of relating to our parents. Unfortunately, for many of us, this often looks the same way it did when we were teenagers. We get annoyed about the same things. We get frustrated with the same things. And we respond the same way we did when we were kids.

The great news is we are able to change this! If you find yourself getting annoyed with that one thing your parent does that just drives you crazy, you can choose to bless instead.

One of our good friends, Marci, and her husband, Jackson, shared their story with me the other day. Marci and Jackson were spending time watching a football game with Jackson's parents. In Seattle, the Seahawks are a way of life, and Jackson's family frequently hosts big events for all their family, neighbors, and friends to attend. During these Seahawks events, the game is blaring, kids are running around, and it's borderline chaos and mayhem.

Jackson's dad is pretty hard of hearing, and communicating with him in a quiet setting can sometimes be a challenge. However, during one of these gatherings, it is virtually impossible.

But this particular day, during the game and even during commercials, Jackson's dad kept asking his son questions. Questions about his life, his job, his interests, his new car, his latest home project—you name it. Jackson would answer, but because of the volume of the game, the size of the crowd, and his hearing loss, Jackson's dad would inevitably have to ask him to repeat his answer.

After about the third round of this, Jackson's replies began to get shorter and snippier. By the end of the first quarter, he had even started to pretend that he didn't hear the questions his dad was asking.

During halftime, Marci pulled her husband aside. "Honey, can I share something with you?" she asked, hoping that between the full plate of nachos in his left hand and an overflowing plate of wings in his right, he would stop chewing long enough to hear her heart.

"Sure, my love," Jackson replied with a smile.

"Well, I've been watching you and your dad the whole game . . ." She paused nervously. "And, Jackson, I think you are really missing the fact that your dad is trying very hard to bless you."

When Jackson didn't say anything, Marci continued. "I know you get really frustrated having to repeat yourself, but, honey, he really can't hear you. And I've watched him patiently and expectantly ask you question after question, even when you've been short or rude to him. But now you are just ignoring him, and you can tell he's hurt, and he was really trying to connect with you."

At this point in the conversation, Jackson had put down both plates of food. Then Marci gently grabbed his hands.

"I know this probably isn't easy to hear, but just last week you were saying that you wished you and your dad talked more. He's literally trying to give you exactly what you've been praying for, but you can't see it because of your frustration. Jackson, you are an amazing husband, son, and father. I just don't want you to miss this moment."

Jackson wiped tears from his eyes and asked his wife, "What do I do about it? You're right. I was getting frustrated. And he was trying to connect with me. But now he's stopped asking me questions."

"Honey, all you have to do is start asking him some questions in return," Marci said with a smile.

The rest of the second half wasn't about football. It was about Jackson and his dad communicating and relating with each other.

Marci watched them with happy tears in her eyes, and everyone in the room could feel the joy in her husband's and father-in-law's hearts—joy that went far beyond any Seahawks win. This day marked a huge shift in Jackson and his dad's relationship—all because Jackson was willing to see that his frustration was blocking his father's attempt to bless and connect with him.

Remember, it's okay if this chapter is either hard or uncomfortable for you. Keep pressing in. Get more support. And keep choosing to bless.

Blessing Activity

Brainstorm some of your own ideas for blessing your parents (or in-laws), or steal one or more of the ideas you liked from the chapter and add your own spin. Set a date and time to give this blessing to your parents (or in-laws).

Making the Blessing a Lifestyle

Use the categories below as a way to come up with your own blessing ideas for your parents (or in-laws). Remember, you do not need to fill in all the blanks, but do try to fill in at least three ideas total.

Don't forget to do this twice—once for each of your parents, if that's an option.

1. What are some activities/hobbies/passions that your parent enjoys? (e.g., cars, football, reading, running, painting)

2. What are some things you have done in the past that have blessed your parent? If you haven't done anything like this before, is there something you can remember your parent appreciating when someone else did it for them? (e.g., made dinner, cleaned the garage, filled up the gas tank, washed the car)

3. What are some big things that your parent has coming up in the next few months? (e.g., a birthday, a presentation at work, a run, a tough day—like the anniversary of a parent's death or divorce)

4. What are some things that you really love and appreciate about your parent? (e.g., they are really caring, good with the budget, a hard worker, funny, full of positivity)

5. What are some things that your parent is struggling with? (e.g., Are they feeling discouraged about what's going on at work? Are they feeling lonely? Does your parent feel like they need to add in some healthy habits but can't seem to find the time?)

6. What is something tangible that your parent really likes (such as their favorite food, drink, or way to celebrate)?

7. Other:

Look at the three things from these categories that you've written.

Next to each item, brainstorm and write down at least one way that you can turn each of those ideas into a blessing.

Finally, take each of the blessing ideas you've written above and add them to your reminders or calendar. Do one blessing a week for three weeks.

CHAPTER 15

Your Next Step Is Living
the Blessing

When is the end a beginning? We pray you've had an encouraging, meaningful, life-building time working through the material in this book. But what's next? Here are several things we'd recommend for you to keep moving forward in giving and living the Blessing. Because, again, it's not just a one-and-done thing.

We mentioned earlier that a great starting place for giving your Blessing is taking part in the Blessing Day. This is a worldwide challenge that we pray and really encourage you to participate in. Using what you've learned in this book, you can put it into action by choosing a Blessing Day. Any day that works best for you and the one you're blessing. We can't encourage you enough to have your own Blessing Day and to join with and encourage others to do a Blessing Day too.

For example, one small group went through the Blessing book but then set up a "go to the park day" where they all brought their kids. The kids didn't know it, but that was about to be their Blessing Day. After playing and eating lunch, the group headed out to different areas in the park. Then they sat down and read their children their blessing. Afterward, they all returned to the tables for cake and a Blessing Day celebration.

We've seen people do this with sports teams where each child gets a blessing. Or even entire churches setting up video cameras where people can tape their blessing and send it to a loved one. So start with your own Blessing Day—and help change lives by encouraging others to do the same as well. Just visit StrongFamilies. com/theblessingday to get started.

Second, pick out a *second place* where you'll start showing up and blessing people. Your home needs to be the first place where you live out the Blessing. But if you're asking, "What's next?" a great thing to do is to step into a second place. For example, there may be a senior citizen's home nearby. Go over and meet with the staff, and see if they need volunteers to encourage, read to, or bless some of the residents. Yes, you might have to go through a background check (as you would if working with children today), and it might seem inconvenient, but there are so many lonely people in these homes who never get a visitor. If you just show up and start looking for ways to speak into their lives, you'll be amazed to see what the Blessing can do in a place where people are often losing hope and longing for someone to love them like Jesus.

Serving seniors is just one option. You could also volunteer at a school or church. We know of one group that worked through the material in this book and then volunteered with their church's children's ministry. Week after week, they stood at the door and gave a quick blessing to each child before the kids headed out of the room and back to Mom and Dad. It became a favorite thing for the children—they would line up, get their blessing, and then run out to Mom and Dad all fired up and talking about the blessing they got. This led to some great talks with parents, and a whole church started learning to bless—all because a few people stood at the door and blessed kids before they ran out.

Be creative and pray for doors to open to start living out the Blessing. Again, the first place to bless is at home, but be looking for that second place as well.

Third, bring a Blessing speaker to your church to launch a Blessing Day Challenge. At StrongFamilies.com you can find out how to bring one of our Blessing speakers to your church, men's event, women's event, or even workplace event.

Fourth, get a Blessing Coach or choose to become a StrongFamilies-certified Blessing and Attachment Coach. Alongside the tremendous ministry at ICCI (International Christian Coaching Institute), Kari and I train people to be LifeMapping Coaches, Strengths Coaches, and Blessing and Attachment Coaches. These are both Life Coaches and those doing "people helping" in their church, ministry, or workplace who want more training on helping people get and give the Blessing, understanding their unique God-given strengths, and building a LifeMap to help them get unstuck and move toward God's best. Learn more at StrongFamilies.com.

Finally, look for webinars, tools, great ideas from others, and more at StrongFamilies.com, the world headquarters of people wanting to live and give the Blessing. Whatever you do, keep moving forward in blessing others and in finding out more about how Jesus can bless your life as well.

Notes

Chapter 2: The Lifelong Search for the Blessing

1. Sue Johnson and Kenny Sanderfer, *Created for Connection* (New York: Little, Brown and Company, 2016).

2. An excellent book we recommend that deals with the impact family influences can have on both the creation and cure of substance abuse is Jeff VanVonderen, *Good News for the Chemically Dependent* (Nashville: Thomas Nelson, 1985).

3. Richard A. McCormisk, "Affective Disorders Among Pathological Gamblers Seeking Treatment," *American Journal of Psychiatry* 141, no. 2 (1984): 215.

Chapter 3: A Life-and-Death Choice

1. See the definition for *live* in Francis Brown, S. R. Driver, and Charles A. Briggs, eds., *A Hebrew and English Lexicon of the Old Testament* (Oxford: Clarendon Press, 1974), 311. See along with James Strong, *Strong's Exhaustive Concordance of the Bible* (Peabody, MA: Hendrickson Publishers), citation 2416. The word *life* carries definitions such as "to be quickened," "running," "springing," and to "troop." We are "alive" when we are animated to "get moving" and, like a "troop" of soldiers, move or step toward an objective.

2. Brown, Driver, and Briggs, *Hebrew and English Lexicon*, 559. *Death* carries the idea of "to depart, to remove, to step away." The New Testament word for *death, thanatos*, also carries this idea of stepping away.

3. Brown, Driver, and Briggs, 139.

4. Brown, Driver, and Briggs, 457. *Honor* carries the idea of "to be heavy, weighty, honored." The idea of coins on a scale can even be seen in one way this word is translated: as an "offering."

5. Brown, Driver, and Briggs, 886b. *Curse* carries the idea of "to be slight, of water, be abated." To see a picture of this in Scripture, go to Genesis 8:3, where the flood waters are "cursed," literally meaning, "the waters abated." It is, in part, pulling away life-giving water from someone when we curse them.

Chapter 4: The First Element: Appropriate Meaningful Touch

1. Job 41:15–17; see also Brown, Driver, and Briggs, *Hebrew and English Lexicon*, 621.

2. Robert E. Salt, "Affectionate Touch," *Journal of Marriage and Family* vol. 53, no. 3 (August 1991), 545.

3. Salt, 545.

4. Salt, 545.

5. The blessing of Ephraim and Manasseh also had a unique spiritual message. When Jacob "crossed" his hands and blessed the younger with the older son's blessing, it was a picture of God's election.

6. Charles F. Pfeiffer, Howard F. Vos, and John Rea, eds., *Wycliffe Bible Encyclopedia* (Chicago: Moody Press, 1975), 750.

7. Harvey Richard Schiffman, *Sensation and Perception: An Integrated Approach* (New York: John Wiley & Sons, 1982), 107.

8. Dolores Krieger, "Therapeutic Touch: The Imprimatur of Nursing," *American Journal of Nursing* 75, no. 5 (May 1975): 784.

9. "We need four hugs a day for survival. We need eight hugs a day for maintenance," says Virginia Satir, noted family therapist and author, quoted in *UCLA Monthly*, Alumni Association News, March–April 1981, 1.

10. Marianne D. Borelli and Patricia Heidt, *Therapeutic Touch* (New York: Springer Publishing, 1981), quoted in *Reader's Digest*, January 1992, 21.

11. Tiffany Field, Touch Research Institute at University of Miami School of Medicine, quoted in "A Conversation on Touch in Early Development," *Current Health* 13, no. 2 (1986): 13.

12. Saul Schanberg and Steven Butler, *Symbiosis in Parent-Offspring Interactions* (New York: Plenum Press, 1983), 41.

13. L. W. Linkous and R. M. Stutts, "Passive Tactile Stimulation Effects on the Muscle Tone of Hypotonic Developmentally Delayed Young Children," *Perceptual and Motor Skills* 71, no. 3, part 1 (December 1990): 951–54.

14. F. B. Dresslar, "The Psychology of Touch," *American Journal of Psychology* 6, no. 3 (1984): 316.

15. Marcia Mark and Perla Werner, "Agitation and Touch in the Nursing Home," *Psychological Reports* 64, no. 3, part 2 (1989): 1020.

16. Mark and Werner, "Agitation and Touch," 1023.

17. Helen Colton, *The Gift of Touch* (New York: Seaview/ Putnam, 1983), 102.

18. Edgar Wycoff and Jill Holley, "Effects of Flight Attendant's Touch upon Airline Passengers' Perceptions of the Attendant and the Airline," *Perceptual and Motor Skills* 71, no. 3, part 1 (December 1990): 932–34.

19. Arthur Janov, "For Control, Cults Must Ease the Most Profound Pains," *Los Angeles Times*, December 10, 1978, part 6, 3.

20. Marc H. Hollender, "The Wish to Be Held," *Archives of General Psychiatry* 22 (1970): 445.

21. Alfred Edersheim, *The Life and Times of Jesus the Messiah, Part Two* (Grand Rapids: Eerdmans, 1972), 329.

22. Sidney Jourard's study, quoted in Tiffany Field, *Touch* (London: Bradford Books, 1988), 22.

Chapter 5: The Second Element: A Spoken or Written Message

1. Gary Smalley, *The Key to Your Child's Heart* (Waco, TX: Word Books, 1984). See the chapter "Balancing Loving Support Through Contracts," 77–107.

Chapter 6: The Third Element: Attaching High Value

1. Brown, Driver, and Briggs, *Hebrew and English Lexicon*, 139.

2. That is why Psalm 95:6 translates the word *bless* as "to bow the knee" when it says, "Come, let us worship and bow down; let us kneel before the LORD our Maker" (literally, "bless him").

3. J. D. Douglas, "Lion of Judah," *New Bible Dictionary* (Grand Rapids: Eerdmans, 1971), 742.

4. Some circles dispute how Solomon, with all his many wives, could be a model for a godly marriage. One can see a commentary on the Song of Solomon for a fuller explanation, but in brief here are two reasons why we feel Solomon's story can still help any married couple today. First, Solomon did not begin to take foreign wives and concubines until later in life, after his visit by the queen of Sheba. Song of Solomon is dated by most scholars as being written early in his reign as king. More important, any person, including Solomon, could leave his first love when he stops walking with God. During Solomon's later years, when he took many wives, his fellowship with God was certainly not where it was when he asked for the gift of wisdom.

5. S. Craig Glickman, *A Song for Lovers* (Downers Grove, IL: InterVarsity Press, 1974), 48.

Chapter 7: The Fourth Element: Picturing a Special Future

1. M. J. Cohen, *The Jewish Celebration Book* (Philadelphia: Jewish Publication Society of America, 1946), 108.

2. Jay Stifler, *The Epistle to the Romans* (Chicago: Moody Press, 1983), 119.

3. We would like to extend our special thanks to Dr. Jeffrey M. Trent, associate professor of medicine, University of Arizona, for putting this example into "everyday English" for us.

Chapter 8: The Fifth Element: An Active, Genuine Commitment

1. For a helpful discussion on this point, see Charles Swindoll, *You and Your Child* (Nashville: Thomas Nelson, 1977), 27–32.
2. Smalley, *Key to Your Child's Heart*, chapter 2, "Expressing Loving Support—The Most Important Aspect of Raising Children."

Chapter 9: Your Blessing Day Begins with a Written Blessing

1. "Dad's Letter Offers Parable for Eldest Daughter," AZCentral, June 3, 1998, http://www.azcentral.com/specials /special25/articles/0603goldwater.html.
2. "Dad's Letter."
3. A personal letter shared with me by the engineer in question.

Chapter 10: Your Blessing

1. "21 Bible Verses About Being Chosen," Knowing Jesus, accessed November 30, 2018, https://bible.knowing-jesus. com/topics/Being-Chosen.
2. "10 Bible Verses That Show Your True Value," accessed November 30, 2018, Amazing Facts, https://www

.amazingfacts.org/news-and-features/news/item/id/13320/t
/10-bible-verses-that-show-your-true-value.

3. Dawn (contributor), "21 Bible Verses for When You Need to Feel God's Love," Seedtime, December 13, 2016, https://christianpf.com/bible-verses-about-gods-love/.

4. Isaiah 43:1 NIV.

5. Isaiah 43:1 NIV.

6. 2 Corinthians 6:18.

7. Romans 8:31–39 NLT.

8. Deuteronomy 31:6.

9. John Callahan, "7 Bible Verses Reminding Us That God Has Given Us a Purpose in Life," Christian Post, accessed November 30, 2018, https://www.christianpost.com/news/7-bible-verses-reminding-us-that-god-has-given-us-a-purpose-in-life-137732.

10. Jeremiah 29:11 NIV.

11. Deuteronomy 30:3–13 THE MESSAGE.

12. Isaiah 42:16 NIV.

13. John 15:16.

14. Luke 15:11–32 NIV.

15. Psalm 139:13–14 NIV.

16. Jeremiah 29:11 NIV.

17. Mark 16:15.

18. John 13:34 NIV.

19. Romans 8:31–39 NLT.

20. John 7:37–38 NIV.

21. Isaiah 40:29–31 NIV.

22. Psalm 30:11–12 NIV.

Chapter 11: Blessing Your Kids and Grandkids

1. "Babies Understand Mother's Tone of Voice Not Their Words," *Telegraph*, January 9, 2012, https://www.telegraph .co.uk/news/health/news/9002249/Babies-understand -mothers-tone-of-voice-not-their-words.html.

2. Lori Kase Miller, "The Benefits of Introducing Baby to Music," *Parents*, October 2014, https://www.parents.com /baby/development/intellectual/the-benefits-of-introducing -baby-to-music/.

3. Joshua A. Krisch, "When Do Babies Understand Facial Expressions?," Fatherly, July 24, 2017, https://www.fatherly .com/health-science/science-facial-expressions/.

4. "What's in a Smile?," Raising Children, July 9, 2015, https:// raisingchildren.net.au/babies/connecting-communicating /bonding/whats-in-a-smile.

Chapter 12: Blessing Your Spouse

1. "Marital Affection: The Foundation for a Healthy Family," *Health Journal*, February 1, 2014, http://www .thehealthjournals.com/marital-affection-foundation-healthy -family/.

2. "Marital Affection."

3. Jenn Morson, "How Much PDA Is Okay in Front of Your Kids?," What to Expect, August 10, 2017, https://www .whattoexpect.com/news/first-year/how-much-pda-okay -front-baby-kids/.

About the Authors

John Trent, PhD, a noted speaker and author, is president of StrongFamilies.com. He and Gary Smalley have won Gold Medallion writing awards for their books *The Blessing* and *The Two Sides of Love*. Dr. Trent has also written "Where Do I Go from Here?" on LifeMapping and several children's books, *including* the Gold Medallion award-winning book on children's personalities, *The Treasure Tree*. Learn more about creating the Blessing culture and lifestyle at StrongFamilies.com.

Gary Smalley was one of the country's best-known authors and speakers on family relationships. In addition to writing *The Blessing* and *The Two Sides of Love* with John Trent, their book *The Language of Love* (newly revised and updated) won the Angel Award as the best contribution to family life. His national infomercial, "Hidden Keys to Loving Relationships," has been viewed by television audiences all over the world.

Kari Trent Stageberg is the CEO of StrongFamilies as well as an author, speaker, and certified Master Coach and Trainer. Kari is committed to helping people experience redemption, love, and blessing through a relationship with Jesus. She has spoken at events and to audiences all over the world, including to more than one million people through Iran Alive Broadcasts. Her story of surviving and healing from domestic violence has been viewed and shared more than a million times. She has written or cowritten *The Blessing*, *The Merge for Marriage*, and *Where Do I Go from Here?*

However, Kari's biggest honor is being married to her incredible husband, Joey, and being a mom to their two young sons.